THE USUAL PATH TO PUBLICATION

27 stories about 27 ways in

Edited by

SHANNON PAGE

PERSONAL ESSAYS BY:

Alma Alexander, Elizabeth Bourne, K. Tempest Bradford,
Chaz Brenchley, Jennifer Brozek, Amy Sterling Casil,
Tina Connolly, Brenda Cooper, Chris Dolley,
Laura Anne Gilman, Rhiannon Held, Randy Henderson,
Jim C. Hines, Katharine Kerr, Mindy Klasky, Trisha Leigh/Lyla
Payne, David D. Levine, Nancy Jane Moore, Ada Palmer,
John A. Pitts, Cherie Priest, Phyllis Irene Radford,
Deborah J. Ross, Ken Scholes, Sara Stamey, Mark Teppo, Jo Walton

The Usual Path to Publication
Edited by Shannon Page
Copyright ©2016

Copy edited by Chaz Brenchley
Cover and interior design by Jane Dixon-Smith

An extension of this copyright page appears on page 143.

ISBN: 978-1-61138-602-8

www.bookviewcafe.com
Book View Café Publishing Cooperative

Dedicated to

The Cascade Writers Workshop Class of 2015
And particularly to Claire Eddy
Thank you for the idea and the encouragement!

CONTENTS

INTRODUCTION

Last summer, during an "ask us anything" panel at the Cascade Writers workshop, an audience member asked the writers to discuss the "usual path to publication." When the bemusement at this impossible question had subsided, we told her that there are as many answers to that as there are published authors. We continued sharing stories all weekend, and by the end of the workshop, this project was born.

In the pages to come, I have collected the *un*usual, amusing, inspirational, bizarre, even dreadful tales of how writers actually got published—and *then* what happened. There are missed connections, dead agents and editors, serendipity, technology woes, ignored advice, and deeply altered expectations; but most of all, there is *persistence*. If one thread unites all the essays in this book, it is that of authors who did not give up.

Though a second thread builds on the first: breaking in is only the start of the adventure. As the publishing landscape continues to change, seemingly faster all the time, established writers are facing canceled series, merging or vanishing houses, agents quitting the business, editors jumping ship, and the bold (and terrifying, and exciting) new world of self-publishing.

Where do we go from here? I'm sure I don't know, in any detail; but I will say with confidence that the authors who stay in the game are the ones who remain as persistent as they had to be to get there in the first place.

I hope you find these collected stories as enjoyable, entertaining, and inspirational as I do!

Shannon Page
February, 2016

HOW I SKIDDED SIDEWAYS
INTO PUBLISHING

Cherie Priest

Technically, my first foray into publishing was an indie-press hot mess. Without going into too much unnecessary and aggravating detail, I got a $300 advance, a lot of broken promises, and a bill on my birthday—from my publisher, who claimed I owed him hundreds of dollars. For reasons.

But let's not dwell on that.

My first real book deal—the one that ultimately launched my career—happened in a round-about fashion that is unlikely to be recreated in the future. I mean, Jesus, I *hope* not, because it partially hinged on the death of an editor.

Oddly, my records suggested that I'd never queried the editor in question, though I *did* receive a form rejection from one of her(?) fellow editors in a different department, at a different imprint under the same publishing umbrella. Who even knows, man. The point is, I had received my official form rejection, and I expected no further contact from this publisher.

~ooo~

(Side Note #1: When I say "form rejection" I mean "the self-addressed, stamped envelope I'd included with a printed copy of

3

the manuscript proposal in question." This was back in the Stone Age, when we did everything via the post office.)

~o0o~

I added the polite thanks-but-no-thanks to my pile of similar rejection slips, and kept trying elsewhere.

Two years passed.

Somewhere in the middle of those two years, I rashly signed my soul away for $300 and the promise of glory, which worked out Not So Well, as you may recall from my first paragraph.

But yes, two years passed from the form rejection…and then one day I was sitting at work, checking emails when I should've been doing something marginally more productive. Lo and behold, a message popped up with a tor.com return address. This message had a subject line that read (something along the lines of), "I hope you're still checking this email." Confused, intrigued, and wary…I clicked that subject line.

And then I was full of light. Joy. Delighted bafflement.

For I had received an email from a real live editor! An assistant editor, actually (at the time, I believe). But a real editor! From a real publisher! Sure, it was a real publisher that had sent me a form rejection, some two years ago…but who cared? Glory be, somehow they'd circled back around!

According to this email, the interested editor had sent a letter asking to chat with me about my book, but the letter had come back undeliverable. The editor had then tried to call me, but my phone number had changed.

~o0o~

(Side Note #2: This was the Stone Age, remember? If you moved, you lost your land-line phone number. Almost no one had a cell phone.)

~oOo~

Finally, she'd tried the email address on my query's header.

I'd only included my email as a lark. At the time, there was actually some debate as to whether including an email address was considered "professional" when it came to queries. My own email started with "cmpriestess" and was…well, it was not the most professional thing on earth, I confess. But I'm eternally glad that I included it, anyway.

At any rate, this lovely assistant editor and a friend had been tasked with cleaning out the office of an editor who had sadly passed away. If I remember correctly, my proposal packet had been in a box, under the desk of the deceased. The assistant editor who had improbably pulled me from the deepest, most unlikely slush pile you can imagine…was the inimitable Liz Gorinsky. I was her first official acquisition as an editor in her own right, and she was my first real editor.

We still work together today.

* * *

Cherie Priest is the author of 19 books and novellas, most recently *I Am Princess X*, *Chapelwood*, and the Philip K. Dick Award nominee *Maplecroft*; but she is perhaps best known for the steampunk pulp adventures of the Clockwork Century, beginning with *Boneshaker*. Her works have been nominated for the Hugo and Nebula awards for science fiction, and have won the Locus Award (among others)—and over the years, they've been translated into nine languages in eleven countries. Cherie lives in Chattanooga, TN, with her husband and a small menagerie of exceedingly photogenic pets.

DON'T TRY THIS AT HOME
OR
THIS CAN ONLY WORK ONCE...

Alma Alexander

So, then. Way back sometime in the last century I wrote this massive doorstop of a fantasy novel (250,000 words. MINIMUM.) I quite liked the beast, but I was an unpublished newbie with no record and—well—a quarter million words of fantasy. Yike.

I don't even remember if I shopped it myself—those were the days, and I might have been young and naïve enough to try—but at some point I discovered, in an Acknowledgments section of a Guy Gavriel Kay book (well, he wrote EXACTLY the kind of thing I wanted to write, so I was looking), the name of his agent. She was a Name, and she worked at one of the most high-faluting, most traditional, most hidebound "old money" agencies in London.

So, I happened to be in London not long after I had completed the monster novel. I also happened to know someone who owned a printer and who was willing to print out the entire manuscript for me. Yes, on paper. I carried it out of there in a box.

I took that box, and I hightailed it straight to the high-faluting, traditional, hidebound "old money" agency. And informed the receptionist in the plush waiting area that I was there to see Agent. Guy Gavriel Kay's agent. The one from the Acknowledgments.

The well-trained receptionist took one look at this fresh-faced ingénue and her box and said, "She's in a meeting."

"That's okay," I said brightly. "I'll wait."

And I parked myself and my box in a chair in the front office.

The receptionist kept on typing something, and casting occasional glances my way—and the glances grew increasingly frequent, and increasingly frustrated. Finally she couldn't handle it any more and she shoved back her chair and stalked off through a door back into some office fastness to which I had no access.

She returned in a short while with another woman in tow. The woman, improbably, was the agent I had come there to see. She must have been nonplussed enough by the story of the twit in the waiting room to come out and see if I was real. I rose from my chair, took my box with both hands, tottered over to her and thrust it into her arms.

"I have a book," I said, smiling.

She was so utterly astonished by this whole exchange that she ACTUALLY WENT AWAY AND READ IT. She phoned me at my London hotel the next day, having read it, and talked to me about it for a bit—but the upshot was that she informed me (not without an odd note of almost regret) that she was in the process of retiring and was trying to shed, rather than add, clients.

Well, nothing came of that, and eventually I got that book published anyway through other channels (it turned out to be the "Changer of Days" duology, out in the USA as *The Hidden Queen* and *Changer of Days*, split into two books at the publisher's whim, with the first part ending on a huge cliffhanger which it was never my intention to put there—you were supposed to carry on reading the next chapter immediately, not need a whole new novel...) And things ticked along for a little while, and life happened, and I got married and moved to the States in the early years of this millennium...and in the fullness of time I wrote another book, another whopper in fact, *The Secrets of Jin Shei* (another 200,000 words, right there).

And I did another obnoxious thing.

I emailed the agent, THAT agent, and I began my note with, "Hi, you probably don't remember me but…"

She emailed me back immediately. With the rather predictable "Of course I remember you." (I don't think she had many people try that trick with her…) But if she was on the verge of retiring when we first met, she was pretty much there now, and she was still not taking on clients. But she knew of a New York agent who might be interested. I asked if I could use her name. She didn't seem surprised at the question, and gave her gracious permission.

I sent the manuscript of *Jin Shei* to the New York agent. She phoned me three days later. The book sold in Italy within three months of her taking it on, and then in the States for an amount of money that made my eyes water.

There were other adventures, after. But that is how I waded into the deeper waters.

I walked into a London literary agency, demanded to see the agent of my choice, and thrust a box of paper into her hands with the words "I have a book." Improbably, instead of taking me by the ear and marching me out of there like the impertinent child that I was, she decided that such chutzpah needed a reward. I'll always be grateful to her for the sheer grace with which she handled the whole thing…and quite literally for the gift of launching a career.

But this could probably only work once. This is a fairy tale. Once upon a time in Old London…

* * *

Alma Alexander's life so far has prepared her very well for her chosen career. She was born in a country which no longer exists on the maps, has lived and worked in seven countries on four continents (and in cyberspace!), has climbed mountains, dived in coral reefs, flown small planes, swum with dolphins, touched two-thousand-year-old tiles in a gate out of Babylon. She is a novelist, anthologist and short story writer who currently shares her life between the Pacific Northwest of the USA (where she lives with her husband and two cats) and the wonderful fantasy worlds of her own imagination. You can find out more about Alma on her website (www.AlmaAlexander.org), or her Facebook page (https://www.facebook.com/pages/Alma-Alexander/67938071280).

MAPPING UNCHARTED TERRAIN
OR
HOW I GOT HERE (THOUGH I'M NOT SURE WHERE "HERE" IS)

Mark Teppo

Back when I was small and more prone to hyperbolic ideas, I woke up one morning thinking about blowing a city up in the first chapter of my yet-unwritten first novel. Now, a few days prior to that morning, I had been told that young writers—especially ones like myself who no one knew—had to announce themselves within a few paragraphs. "Image you're standing in line at the grocery store and you've got a few minutes to scan the racks of paperbacks," I had been told. "You pick one at random. You read the first page. What is going to hook you enough that you'll keep reading, that you'll put the book in your cart and take it home?"

I'm going to blow up a city, is what I thought. *Page one. That'll show them. There won't be a book left on the racks.*

What had woken me that morning was the realization that I didn't have a good plan for the other three hundred and twenty pages of that book. Also, what do you do for a climax when you've already leveled a couple hundred city blocks? And what if the publisher wants a sequel?

~oOo~

That morning was twenty-five years ago now. Most grocery stores don't even stock paperbacks anymore, and if they do, they're far away from the cash registers.

~oOo~

Eventually, I did write that book, but the big explosion was moved to the climax. I also wrote a sequel; or rather, I wrote five complete drafts of a book that was supposed to be the sequel, but I wasn't a very good editor. Instead of fixing books, I thought it was easier to write them from scratch. This fallacy arose because I was a fast writer. The draft of the first book was done in fifty-six days. I don't know why I still remember that detail; perhaps because I still dream of writing a book that fast again.

Anyway, that book was titled *Souls of the Living*, and it featured a protagonist who was both a vampire AND a werewolf, because, as I mentioned earlier, I was prone to hyperbolisms. The time was 1992—maybe 1993. Jim Butcher's Harry Dresden books weren't going to happen for nearly a decade yet. Laura K. Hamilton's Anita Blake series started in 1993. I was ahead of the curve, which probably explains many of the rejections that book received.

"Thanks, but we're not doing horror."

"Thanks, but we're a SF publisher; we don't do suspense novels."

"The author really thinks highly of himself, as is evidenced by his stand-in main character."

"We don't know what to do with this book."

My agent, who was a junior junior agent working out of the broom closet at Writers' House, called and asked: "Well, what else are you working on?"

"A sequel," I said.

"That's nice," she said, and a year later, when she left the agency, they dropped me.

The time was now 1996—maybe 1997. I had managed to get one story published. Well, "bought." The publisher canceled the publication shortly after my story was acquired. The story was later collected into an anthology of lost stories that had been cast adrift by the termination of the magazine. I don't recall being paid.

~oOo~

Nearly twenty years later, that story, "A Christmas Wish," gets called "superb" by *Publishers Weekly* in their review of my first collection, *The Court of Lies*. I'm only lying a little when I say none of the words had been changed in the intervening two decades.

~oOo~

I did what any author in their mid-twenties who thought they had a brain of fire would do in the face of such rejection: I took my toys and went home.

The millennium came and went, and the world didn't come to an end. I got older and grayer. A bit wider, too. The brain fire went out, though there was a coal that refused to die. Eventually, I got tired of it slowly burning a hole in the back of my brain and I started writing again. I got myself a website, because that was what new writers did: they got themselves a web presence. I started "live journaling," which is to say, I started talking about nothing of import to twelve other people who were as eager to be discovered as was I.

I pulled out the manuscript to *Souls of the Living*, as well as the box with all five versions of *Hunter of Souls*, and I shook my head at the foolishness of rewriting instead of editing. Not that I knew how to do the former, yet.

And nothing happened.

Until I remembered that I had put up a contact email on my website that was not my day-to-day email address. I went and checked that inbox, and found it full of penis spam and people wanting me to buy watches. I deleted all of it, but as this was all still a novelty (*ooh! spam!*), I actually read a few of the emails that looked like they might be from real people. And one email was really good at pretending to be a human being. It talked about my writing and that I had written a book, and blah blah blah...

Suddenly, I realized—*holy shit!*—this guy has actually read *Souls of the Living*!

He had been an intern at one of the large publishing houses, and had really wanted his boss to buy the book. He explained to me that when he had finished school and gone out into the world, he and a pal had opened up a literary agency and were building their client list. He remembered the book from back in the day when he had been fresh-faced and eager, and he had been surprised to discover that the book had never been published. *It's a shame*, he wrote, *that book should be out there!*

Naturally, I was totally seduced by this outpouring of love for my words, and I signed with this agency.

However, I had read *Souls* in the interim. "I have one condition," I told my new agent, "I want to do a top to bottom rewrite of the book. A 21st century reconditioning."

"But, but, but," they said, "we like the book the way it is."

"The protagonist is a vampire AND a werewolf," I said. "And the author was an angry twenty-five-year-old man child who had some shit to work out. I can fix this."

And by *fix*, I mean, throw out every word and write the book from scratch.

I kept the Chorus. And the character names. And the setting. And the big explosion in the end.

I rewrote the book, and it became *Lightbreaker*. Guess what? Those five versions of the sequel? Totally worthless. Nothing could be salvaged…though I might still use the crucifixion on the golden arches of a McDonald's sign somewhere.

After I turned in the book and my agents agreed that the new version was the right choice, they wanted me to come out to Madison, WI, for the World Fantasy Convention that was taking place there that year. *This is the big time*, my agents said. *This is where all the deals happen. It's not like the small local conventions.*

I nodded, and dimly recalled being a part of World Horror in Eugene, OR, a hundred years ago or so. Or—what was the name of that convention in Bellingham, WA—*VikingCon*? Hadn't I moderated a panel there with a bunch of hard SF guys, including the guest of honor?

Different times. Different writer.

My agents made contact with their editor of choice at the convention, and the book went on its merry way.

And then we waited.

That was the fall of 2005.

I worked on the sequel to *Lightbreaker*, because I still hadn't learned the lesson from that conversation with my Writers' House agent a decade previously. Along the way, I had an idea for a short story. I wrote it in an afternoon, and mailed it off before I over-thought what I had just done. Several months later, it sold, and in early 2007, "How the Mermaid Lost Her Song" became my first professional sale. It's not even 1,500 words, but *Strange Horizons* was a SFWA recognized market, and a sale was a sale.

This sale started the clock for the John W. Campbell Award for Best New Writer. I had two years of eligibility, but I didn't have a bunch of stories waiting to go out. The novel was still sitting on the desk of our top choice for editor in New York, and it was going to be there awhile, we thought.

It's hard to sit and wait when the clock is ticking.

~oOo~

Through my agent, I met a few of the other new writers in the list and we bonded. Bonding is good, especially when you're all waiting for something to happen. One of these people was Darin Bradley, and he founded Farrago's Wainscot, a webzine devoted to the weird and experimental. He knew I was eager to do something, and so he asked if there was anything I wanted to do for Old Man Farrago.

I suggested a dream journal of hyperlinked ideas. I'd become aware of a proclivity to use the same words again and again in my writing, and I was curious to see what sort of strange mapping could happen between these common words. I pitched a narrative excuse for this mapping, and we decided to run this "dream journal" in monthly installments during the first year at Farrago's. It would be called *The Oneiromantic Mosaic of Harry Potemkin*. I started writing it in September of 2006. The first section was supposed to go up in January of 2007, with new content following every thirty days.

Each month during that year, I wrote for two weeks and then spent the remaining two weeks doing web layout and re-linking of the content. Because when you do a hypertext project and add content to it, you have to include existing links in the new content and new links in the existing content. You have to re-map the whole thing every month. For our readers, every month, there would be new paths through the narrative. It would be nearly impossible to follow the path you took the previous month, unless you kept a long history file in your browser.

What the hell were we thinking?

Well, there was a secondary goal that I wanted from this project. I had written five drafts of the second book, remember? I was getting pretty good at recognizing when a book went off the rails, but I still didn't know how to fix an existing draft. I always bailed and started over. I figured if I was writing in public, I couldn't bail. I couldn't start over. I had to figure the story out.

The *Mosaic* ran twelve months. It's around 120,000 words. And I had no idea where it was going when I started it.

But I nailed the ending.

~oOo~

Somewhere along the way—during late summer, perhaps—I got THE CALL. The first editor had finally passed on *Lightbreaker*, and my agents had sent it out to a handful more people. One night, I got a call from a publisher I knew, and the first thing he said to me was: "Holy shit, dude. You can write. I mean, I've been drinking with you for several years, and I know you can do that. But, damn, you can actually write too!"

"So I guess you liked *Lightbreaker*, then?" I asked, feigning indifference, because this was how the game was played.

He did, and made an offer on the book.

Almost immediately thereafter, the publisher ran into financial trouble, and the actual release of *Lightbreaker* was delayed long enough that I'm not sure anyone remembers exactly when it showed up on the shelf. Online records say 2007; the copyright page says 2008; I recall it was early 2009 or so.

Somewhere in there, my eligibility for the John W. Campbell Award for Best New Writer ran out, probably before anyone could actually purchase my first novel.

Heartland, the sequel to *Lightbreaker*, wandered into stores at some point in 2010, just in time for Borders to decide to send back all of their copies—along with the copies of hundreds of other books by other authors, of course; it's not all about me. I'm not too broken up that folks might have missed the sequel. Those were trying times for bookstores.

~oOo~

Lightbreaker is being re-released by the new iteration of Night Shade Books in March of 2016. This edition will be my twelfth or fifteenth book, depending on how you want to count them. It remains the first novel-length idea I ever had, twenty-five years ago.

And it's still the only esoteric magick ritual masquerading as an urban fantasy book out there.

Writing is waiting.

And while you're waiting, keep tending the fire in your brain. It's the light that guides you and keeps you warm as you travel through uncharted territory.

* * *

Mark Teppo is the author of a dozen novels that run the gamut across historical adventure fiction, eco-thrillers, urban fantasy, and experimental narrative. His latest effort at subverting genre conventions is to build his own publishing company, Resurrection House. He finally figured out how to replicate the hypertext experience of *The Potemkin Mosaic* in a print volume format.

TWO PATHS

Laura Anne Gilman

There are two stories I could tell—the story of my first novel sale, or my first *original* novel sale. They're both...not exactly traditional.

My first novel sale came out of fanfiction. I had been talking to a friend of mine who was, like me, heavy into the Buffy fandom, and I'd been telling him about the fanfic I was working on in between the (original) short stories I'd been selling. And he stopped me and said (paraphrased), "Don't write that as fic. That's a good idea. Send it as a proposal to Lisa (the editor of the official BtVS tie-in novels)."

I scoffed, because tie-in projects aren't given to untried novelists, no matter how good the idea. They want established professionals they can rely on. But when I mentioned this to another friend, who *was* an established novelist, she said, "So we'll write it together."

And we did. And they bought it (and another one). And that's why I eyeroll when people claim that "pros" don't write fanfiction.

But there was only so far I could go, writing in someone else's world, with all the restrictions of the form. So I kept working on my original fiction. Got an agent. Had the agent send out what we thought was the strongest of my works, a historical fantasy. Got lots of "this is really well-written, but..."

I was sad. I was depressed. I was grumpy af. I started working on something completely different, which I didn't think would ever sell, either.

Around then, I went out to lunch with a fellow editor, who was starting up a new fantasy imprint focusing on strong female characters with a hard emphasis on historical and epic settings. She had my historical fantasy under submission, and hadn't rejected it yet—but we were lunching editor-to-editor, not editor-to-writer, so I didn't mention it. And then, at the end of lunch, my friend said, "So what else are you working on?"

"An urban fantasy"—mind, this is back when UF was still considered dead as the proverbial doornail—"with a caper-mystery plot, set in NYC."

"Cool," she said. "Why don't you send that to me, too?"

"But you aren't buying UF."

She shrugged. I had my agent send it.

Time passed. Months, not years, thankfully. I was on vacation with my family in Italy, with no cell phone access (no cell phone, back then) when I got an email from my agent.

They'd made an offer for the urban fantasy. For the genre they weren't originally buying. Three books.

I think my yell echoed all the way back to NYC.

* * *

Since her first novel in 2004, Laura Anne Gilman has established a reputation for herself with darker-edged fantasy, both urban and epic. She is the author of the bestselling *Silver on the Road*, Book 1 of *The Devil's West,* the Nebula-nominated *The Vineart War* trilogy, and the long-running *Cosa Nostradamus* series, plus more than forty short stories, including two "Year's Best" picks. Her story collection, *Darkly Human*, will be out from Book View Café in 2016. Currently based in Seattle, she's on Twitter as @LAGilman, and at http://www.lauraannegilman.net.

THE GOBLIN'S CURSE

Jim C. Hines

Back at the turn of the century, I was a struggling young writer, submitting stories and collecting rejection letters and digging up all the writing-related information I could find on the handful of primitive writing-related online bulletin boards, waiting for each topic to creep onto the screen through my 56K modem. I was a turbo-charged vacuum sponge, sucking up every scrap of advice and guidance.

Unfortunately, I was a little too indiscriminate in my sponging. Everyone's path is unique. Writing and publishing evolve. The rules today are very different from the rules when I broke in. Likewise, the maps people followed in the '70s, '80s, and '90s weren't necessarily the best for navigating the publishing labyrinth of 2000.

"Short fiction you must publish first," the wise old authors said. "A reputation you must create. Only then, a novelist can you become."

Once upon a time, that was probably good advice. And for years, I followed it. I set novel-length ideas aside and tried to write and sell short stories. After a lot of rejection, I finally made some semi-pro sales, and then eventually a pro sale. Then another story won *Writers of the Future*. Go me!

Holding those magazines and anthologies with my work in them was awesome, but I wanted more. So I began writing novels, each time trying to write a masterful piece of beautifully crafted, emotionally powerful, award-worthy fiction. The kind of books I thought I *should* be writing. The stories my research suggested were most likely to give me that big breakthrough.

None of them really went anywhere.

Feeling frustrated and stuck and burnt out, I finally joined a handful of friends in a novel dare, writing a full 80,000+ words in a single month. For just one month, I disregarded the advice, I said the heck with what I *should* be writing, and I had fun. I wrote slapstick and cannibalism jokes and invented a spider who sets things on fire.

I didn't expect it to sell. On the other hand, what did it hurt to try? I sent the book out to the handful of publishers that took unsolicited manuscripts, and I began collecting rejections. And then, figuring maybe I just hadn't done enough short fiction yet to be ready for novels, I went back to the short stories.

I sold a few more. I did some clumsy networking, and managed to get a few anthology invitations. I even got a story into Esther Friesner's fourth Chicks anthology, *Turn the Other Chick*. That's where things took an interesting twist.

Friesner edited the Chicks anthologies, but Martin H. Greenberg's company Tekno Books did the actual packaging of the collection. The individual at Tekno who helped with *Turn the Other Chick* was also the SF/F acquiring editor for a small, library-oriented publisher called Five Star Books.

By now, it was a year and a half since I'd finished *Goblin Quest*. Most places had sent form rejections. A few hadn't responded at all. So I queried the editor at Five Star and asked if he'd be interested in a book about a goblin getting dragged into a fantasy quest.

He said yes.

A short time later, he said he wanted to buy the book.

Five Star was a small press, so they didn't pay a huge advance, but it was an advance. It was an acceptance. It was an offer to turn *Goblin Quest* into a REAL, LIVE BOOK! With a cover and pages and everything!

Just to be safe, I emailed the last couple of publishers who'd never gotten back to me and let them know I was withdrawing the manuscript. I then emailed Five Star to accept their offer.

Life was good.

In late 2004, Five Star released a hardcover edition of *Goblin Quest*, targeted at the library market.

Jump ahead a few months to very early 2005. Remember those big publishers who'd never gotten back to me? One of them got back to me. With an offer to buy the book. The book that had already been sold to a small press. The book that had just been published.

I don't know what happened to my email withdrawing the book. I don't know why it took more than two and a half years to get back to me. (Though I've learned that this is, unfortunately, not unusual for unsolicited manuscripts to the major publishers.)

So I did what any writer who'd spent more than a decade dreaming about an offer from a big publisher would do: I freaked the hell out.

After a while, I calmed down enough to realize Five Star, being library-oriented, didn't do mass market paperbacks. I still owned those rights. Maybe the big publisher could do something with those? Maybe I could still salvage my dream?

I told the publisher the situation. They were disappointed, but said they might be willing to do a deal for just the mass market rights. THERE WAS HOPE!

And then, following the advice of my peers, I started calling around for an agent to represent me. Because everybody knew that once a publisher offered to buy your book, that was the time you called up agents and brought them into the negotiations.

Everybody knew that, except for this particular publisher. What was standard practice elsewhere turned out to be an Unforgivable Sin with this individual. I did manage to find an agent, but as soon as the agent got involved, the publisher stopped returning our phone calls. When the agent finally managed to get the publisher on the phone, the publisher said, "We're withdrawing the offer," and hung up.

I was crushed. I spiraled into depression and despair, and only managed to start to snap out of it when my son was born a few months later.

I had lost my golden ticket, my invitation to be one of the Real Writers. But I still had an agent. They hadn't dumped me when the publisher hung up. Instead, they sold *Goblin Quest* to a Russian publisher. It wasn't the same, but it was still pretty cool. They encouraged me to keep writing. They pointed out that I'd written a book one of the big publishers wanted; that meant I could do it again. All I had to do was sit down and write my next book.

I wasn't sure I believed them, but I tried. I started one book... it didn't go anywhere. I played with another idea...nothing. Finally, in an attempt to keep myself from getting even more depressed and unhappy with my writing "career," such as it was, I went back to the goblins. Writing a sequel to an unsellable book wasn't the best idea, but I loved those goblins, and their antics amused me. I needed fun and light in my life, and they provided it. I tried to make *Goblin Hero* stand on its own as much as I could, and when it was as good as I could make it, I sent it to my agent.

He shopped it around. A little while later, he said two different publishers had expressed interest.

Holy crap! You mean my career wasn't dead? My dream wasn't over? My melodramatic anguish over the end of all that was bright and good in this world was, perhaps, premature?

There was a catch, of course. Both editors noted that while the book was fun, it felt like a second book. Was there, perhaps, more to the story?

I wasn't there to witness this part, but in my mind, I imagine my agent sitting back, cigar in hand, saying, "I love it when a plan comes together," before writing up a cover letter and sending *Goblin Quest* to both editors, offering mass market rights and a lovely two-book deal.

DAW Books bought them both. In 2006, their mass market paperback edition of *Goblin Quest* hit the shelves. As happy as I'd been about working with Five Star, this felt like I'd leveled up. My book was in bookstores. I could walk into Borders and find Jig the goblin looking up at me from the shelves.

Today, I've sold a total of fourteen novels to DAW: three goblin books, four fairy tale retellings, a four-book urban fantasy series, and an as-yet-unwritten SF trilogy. I've written a tie-in novel for another major publisher. I've published more than fifty short stories. I go to conventions, and people—some of them, anyway—actually know who the heck I am!

I'm still with the same agency, too. They continue to negotiate foreign deals for my work, and to help me build my career.

In some ways, I followed a very boring path. I wrote a book, submitted it to a big publisher, got an offer, got an agent, and went on to sell the book. But I could never do things the easy way, and I managed to turn that boring path into a pothole-laden Autobahn. I wiped out repeatedly, crashing and burning and making a right mess of everything.

And yet, it worked out. DAW is an amazing publisher, and a great fit for me and my writing. JABberwocky is a strong literary agency, with an amazing amount of knowledge and insight.

Those months of highs and lows were in many ways a microcosm of what it meant to be a writer. For most of us, this path is anything but stable. There are ups and downs from year to year, month to month, even day to day. (Heck, depending on the day, you can go through a dozen mood swings over the course of an hour.)

You can't control what the editors might say. You can't plot out your writing career based on what worked for other people, especially if those people broke in decades earlier. You can't guarantee success. The highs won't last forever…but neither will the lows.

All you can do is write the next book.

* * *

Jim C. Hines' first novel was *Goblin Quest*, the humorous tale of a nearsighted goblin runt and his pet fire-spider. Actor and author Wil Wheaton described the book as "too f***ing cool for words," which is pretty much the Best Blurb Ever. After finishing the goblin trilogy, he went on to write the Princess series of fairy tale retellings and the Magic ex Libris books, a modern-day fantasy series about a magic-wielding librarian, a dryad, a secret society founded by Johannes Gutenberg, a flaming spider, and an enchanted convertible. He's also the author of the Fable Legends tie-in *Blood of Heroes*. His short fiction has appeared in more than fifty magazines and anthologies. You can find him online at www.jimchines.com.

THAT LONG WINDING ROAD

Katharine Kerr

In 1979, and mark that date well, I started writing a historical novel. I'd already written a "trunk novel," that is, a novel so bad that it lives in a box in my basement, forever unseen by human eyes. I decided that setting a book in a historical period might help me focus my work. I'd spent my later childhood and miserable adolescence in the small California town of Santa Barbara, a location I thus knew well. I also knew that back near the turn of the 20th century, Santa Barbara had sported a successful motion picture studio as well as a lot of very rich people's winter retreats.

Silent film—real silent films, not the jerky stupid parody of them found on TV—was a hobby of mine at the time. Rich people, I figured, would be a good selling point, too, though I had no intention of writing one of those "sex and shopping" things that were so popular in the 1980s.

The characters came alive and took over. By 1981 I'd written a first draft of a very long book that I knew needed a lot of work. While I revised, I researched agents and publishing with books from the public library, a resource that more aspiring writers should know about. Much to my shock, my first choice of agent took on the project, CATCH THE SHADOWS. She made some excellent suggestions for further revisions, which I followed. As she began sending the book out, she made another crucial suggestion: write your next book. Don't get compulsive over this one.

And a damn good thing I followed that advice. While SHADOWS made the rounds of endless rejections, I wrote DAGGERSPELL, the book that launched my career as a fantasy and science fiction author. As for poor SHADOWS, editors thought it was too long, too complicated, not "romantic" enough. The real stumbling block, however, turned out to be one of the main characters. He was sympathetic, warm-hearted, talented, and gay. Back in the early '80s, gay characters in mainstream, "entertainment" books had to be evil and twisted. Or so we were told.

Fast forward to some years later. "Will and Grace" was becoming a huge TV hit. LGBT people were starting to seeking the right to marry. They were becoming respectable at last, and, I hoped, taking that particular character with them. Because I'd learned a lot about writing fiction in the interval, I revised SHADOWS again, and my agent resolutely sent it out. Still no dice. Although my novel had gotten shorter, so had the attention spans of editors, or at least, the editors thought that readers had shorter attention spans. And despite the simmering, brooding, passionate heterosexual love story at its heart, it still wasn't "romantic" enough, even though I never intended the book to be a category Romance. So once again, the book went back on the agent's shelf.

We now come to 2014, some thirty-five years after I began writing the book. My agent and I were both aware that we weren't getting any younger. As one does at that time of life, we began thinking of Things Left Undone. She realized that although she'd read several hundred proposals and nearly as many full books since last touching SHADOWS, she still remembered the characters vividly. "It's worth trying again" was her judgment. I squeezed a few more words out of it and gave it a new title, FLICKERS. Once again we received a barrage of rejections.

And then, the miracle. One of the editors who'd initially rejected the book found himself continuing to think about it. This, apparently, is rare in publishing. He contacted my agent, bullied his Publishing Committee, and lo! we had a contract. I did do a few more revisions thanks to his suggestions, but they were small nips and tucks here and there, not major changes.

FLICKERS, by the pseudonymous Kathryn Jordan, will be available in March, 2016, from the "Lyrical" division of Kensington Books. Thirty-seven years after I began writing it. Sometimes it pays to be stubborn. Even more often, it pays to revise your work.

* * *

Katharine Kerr lives in the San Francisco Bay Area with her husband, two cats, and a vagrant skunk. Although she spent her childhood in a Great Lakes industrial city, she became a confirmed Californian at age nine, when her family relocated here. She's the author of the Deverry series of epic fantasies, the Nola O'Grady series of light-hearted urban fantasy, and a few science fiction works, most notably SNARE.

HOW TO SELL A NOVEL IN ONLY FIFTEEN YEARS

David D. Levine

My idea of the "usual path to publication" was obsolete before I even started.

I grew up reading science fiction. My dad had been an SF reader since he was a kid, and our shelves were packed with SF paperbacks and magazines. I wrote a lot of SF stories in elementary and high school (to the point that my English teachers begged me to write something else) and in college (where I took an SF writing class and several people urged me to submit my work), but when I graduated I wound up working as a technical writer, and writing fiction was too much like the day job. So I didn't write a word of fiction for twenty years, until I switched from technical writing to software engineering. With that change, suddenly my fiction-writing brain came back online. Shortly after that I had a seven-week sabbatical from work, and I decided to use the time to attend Clarion West. I started selling short stories within a year after that.

At the time I thought that the path to publication consisted of 1) make a name for yourself writing short stories, 2) sell a novel (possibly a fix-up of those same stories), 3) profit! That path may have been true in the '30s, '40s, and '50s, when the stories and essays I grew up on had been written, but by the year 2000 it was, in some ways, easier to sell a first novel than to garner significant attention by selling short stories. But I didn't know that at the time.

The Clarion workshops use short stories as a teaching tool—most students write six or more stories during the six weeks—and I found that I enjoyed writing short stories, and people enjoyed reading them. A lot. I won the Writers of the Future Contest and the James White Award in the year after Clarion West, I had stories picked up by a couple of Year's Best anthologies, and I was nominated for the John W. Campbell Award for Best New Writer in both of the years I was eligible. In the second of those years I was also nominated for the Hugo Award for Best Short Story, and two years after that I was nominated again…and won it!

But during this time I also discovered that short stories, even award-winning short stories, were not as significant to the field as they had been in the days of my father's pulp magazines. Most of my SF-reading friends didn't read short stories at all—in those days you had to subscribe to magazines or buy anthologies, they weren't available free on the internet—and I found that even first-time novelists had more name recognition than I did. The end of every year brought a flood of "best SF books of the year" articles, but virtually no attention to short fiction. Novels—even middling-successful novels—had more readers, more reviews, and brought in more money than even the most highly recognized short stories.

So, round about the time of my first Campbell nomination, I decided it was time to sell a novel. I took what seemed to me the best of my novel ideas, drafted and revised it, got feedback (one agent called it "publishable as it stands"), revised it again, and submitted it to an editor at a major publishing house who had been bugging me for years to send him a novel as soon as I had one. He got back to me *one week later* and said he wanted to buy it! I sat back and waited for the contract to land in my mailbox.

And waited. And waited.

It took nearly a year—a year that included much correspondence, solicitation of blurbs from my writer buddies, and a pretty substantial rewrite—before the editor admitted that he simply couldn't convince his publisher to let him buy the book. I was devastated. But, I figured, I had come so close on my first attempt...surely it would sell to someone else.

The editor who hadn't been able to buy my book introduced me to a friend of his at another publishing house, who immediately requested the full manuscript. It was still on his desk when I won the Hugo, and at the party afterward he shook my hand, gave me a thumbs-up, and said "You'll be hearing from us!"

Well, I did hear from them. Eventually. It took eight more months, and the answer was no.

I had managed to get an agent during the year I was expecting a contract Any Day Now from editor #1, and after that second rejection he sent it everywhere...but no one was interested. Most of the rejections were of the "like it, don't love it" variety, but one small-press publisher—someone who had been very impressed with my short stories and encouraged me strongly to submit a novel when I had one—turned it down, with regrets, because it was "too commercial" for his house. I finally had to admit that it just wasn't going to sell. It did have a weird structure (alternating points of view jumping back and forth in time, converging on a single pivotal event in the middle—I figured that if Iain M. Banks could get away with it, so could I) and some very unconventional relationships (in the course of the book the main character slept with men, women, and aliens, sometimes several at once). So while it was receiving rejection after rejection I wrote a second novel. This one, too, was received enthusiastically by the first editor I sent it to but denied by his publisher. (Different editor, same publisher.)

My agent sent the second novel to a couple more publishers, but it too garnered only rejections. This one had a simpler structure (still alternating points of view, but a straightforward time sequence) but it featured a trans-generational lesbian relationship, a psychic rape scene, and the murder of God. I started work on a third novel, this one with only one point of view, a heterosexual relationship, and no problematic religious or philosophical concepts.

Around this time I started to think that maybe my agent wasn't doing as much for me as I wanted. He was only submitting to one publisher at a time, and didn't seem to have any better contacts than I did in the publishing world or to be able to get them to respond any more quickly than I could myself. I talked to another agent at a convention, who said, "I can't talk to you while you are already represented." So I fired my agent and sent the manuscript to her.

She turned me down. So did all of the other agents I contacted.

For several years I kept submitting novel #2, and occasionally novel #1, to both agents and editors. But no editor wanted either one, and very few agents would even consider a novel that had already been shopped at all. Also—and I found this very discouraging—many people, including editors at science fiction publishers, told me that "science fiction just isn't selling these days." I looked at novel #3, which I had just finished—a hard SF novel set on Mars—and decided to shelve the first draft rather than revise it.

At this time I was really discouraged. Even though I was still selling short stories regularly, and getting some good critical attention, I hadn't won an award in a long time and all I had to show for seven years of trying to sell a novel was three manuscripts that no one wanted. I didn't even have an agent any more.

Okay, I thought, if they don't want what I've been trying to sell them, maybe I should try to sell them something else. I looked at my file of novel ideas and picked one that was more fantasy than SF, but had enough SF-like elements that I could enjoy writing it. (I've always written both F and SF, but my heart is really on the SF side of the fence.) I brainstormed the plot with some writer friends, I did a ton of historical research, I got feedback from three different groups at various points, and after two years of work I had a manuscript that I was really excited about. Many people who read it said they liked it a lot. Could this be the one?

Editor #1—the one who had loved my first novel, but hadn't been able to convince his publisher to let him buy it—had never let up, continuing to ask me if I had anything else. He was a bigger wheel at the publisher by now, being responsible for one of their top bestsellers, and I decided to give him another chance. I sent him that fourth manuscript and waited.

And waited. And waited.

While I was waiting, I worked on short stories and pitched novel #4 to agents. The response to this one was somewhat better than to the first two, but was still only nibbles, no actual bites. And then one day the dam broke. In a single week I got not just one, but *three* offers of representation.

The first was a very enthusiastic agent I met via Twitter; he usually represented only non-fiction but was excited by my book. However, he felt it needed some significant rewrites. The second was a big-name agent, a powerhouse in the field. But I would be the smallest fish in his pond, and as he was a sole proprietor I might be left high and dry in case of illness or overwork on his end. The third was a young agent at a very big agency. He didn't have a big reputation or a lot of personal clout, but two of his clients were friends of mine and they liked him.

After talking on the phone with all three, and asking the advice of all my writer friends, I signed with the small guy at the big house. I figured that, of the three of them, he was the most likely to give me the attention I needed, and he and I would have a chance to grow up together.

At this point I'd been waiting nearly nine months for a response from the editor. My agent sent the manuscript to a few other publishers, but didn't want to "go wide" until we heard back from the first editor. He and I both pinged the editor repeatedly. No response.

Finally I ran out of patience. After consulting with my agent, I wrote to the editor: "The one-year anniversary of my submission of this manuscript is coming up in a few weeks. If I don't hear from you by that date, I'm pulling it." No response.

The days ticked by. Still no response. I was certain I'd blown it—with my rash ultimatum I had not only destroyed my chances with this editor, but with this publisher for all time. All the other publishers too. I would have a reputation as an entitled prima donna, no one would ever buy a novel from me, and it was my own damn fault.

And then, on the very last day before my deadline, the editor came through with an offer. For three books.

Rather than the joy I had expected, I felt only a sick sense of relief.

It was a pretty good offer, but my agent negotiated an even better one, and I accepted it. Then came the contract negotiations; this was another place where having an agent, particularly an agent at a big house, was an enormous help. From the markups on the contract, I could see that my agency's legal team had negotiated some beneficial changes that I'm sure I would not only have been unable to get on my own, I wouldn't even have known to ask for. The lawyer also walked me through the contract and answered my questions about what each clause really meant. It took five months before I got a contract, but when it arrived I was so satisfied with it that I literally only asked for one word to be changed before I signed it.

At this writing I have gone through development edits and copy edits, currently have galleys to proof and ARCs in hand, and look forward to a hardcover and ebook release in the middle of next year. I have a fabulous cover and sensational blurbs, and I feel very well treated by my publisher. There have been a few snafus along the way, some of them pretty serious, but they've all been handled and at the moment I feel very positive about my forthcoming release. Also, I'm about three-quarters done with the first draft of the second book in the series. I've never written a sequel before, so this is another new adventure.

I can't say that I regret my fifteen years in the short-story mines. I learned a lot about the craft and business of writing in that time, I made a lot of friends in the industry, I got the personal satisfaction of many honors and awards, and I did build up a bit of name recognition. But even a Hugo for short stories doesn't help as much as you might expect in selling a novel. In the end, the thing that got me a novel sale was writing a damn good novel and getting it in front of the right editor at the right time—just like any other first-time novelist. And, frustrating though it was at the time, I think that writing three unsalable (so far) novels was an important part of that process.

All along the way I've repeatedly said "all I want is a better class of problems," and I've repeatedly gotten my wish. At this point I stand on the threshold of publication, and I know that the most interesting problems are still ahead of me.

I wonder what the next fifteen years will bring?

* * *

David D. Levine is the author of the novel *Arabella of Mars* (Tor 2016) and over fifty science fiction and fantasy stories. His story "Tk'Tk'Tk" won the Hugo Award, and he has been shortlisted for awards including the Hugo, Nebula, Campbell, and Sturgeon. Stories have appeared in *Asimov's*, *Analog*, *F&SF*, numerous Year's Best anthologies, and his award-winning collection *Space Magic*.

IT ALL HAPPENED BECAUSE OF NETSCAPE NAVIGATOR

K. Tempest Bradford

I started down the road to getting published professionally because of an Internet browser. No, really!

Imagine, if you will, the glorious days of the late 1990s when people were still accessing the Internet through dial-up and most of us were doing that through AOL. It was a harrowing time of per-hour charges and really, really slow-loading websites.

Back then companies were still trying to figure out how to leverage the Internet, especially once people started leaving the walled gardens of AOL and CompuServe and other such services. One way they did this was by making deals with Netscape— which not only made a browser but an email program and news reader—to put their content in front of us users. This is how I came across the Del Rey newsletter. It was mixed in amongst a long list of web newsletters Netscape suggested I subscribe to; and I did so, figuring I'd find out about new books and maybe even get a coupon.

Instead, that newsletter told me about something way more valuable: a free online workshop for people who write science fiction and fantasy. *Hey, I write that stuff!* I thought. And I wanted to get better.

At the time I was in college and had been writing seri- ously since high school. I'd joined some other online writing communities (including some on AOL) and received a bit of feedback from my peers. None of it was consistent, though. The Del Rey Online Writing Workshop (OWW for short) seemed to be the place to get that consistent feedback and give some. Once I signed up, I found the OWW's mailing list where other members were chatting away about writing, about the SFF community, and about other random stuff.

That mailing list changed everything for me.

The workshop itself was important, of course. However, without the accompanying community, I'm not sure I would have gotten as much out of it. I met and made friends with people who sought out and critiqued my fiction when I posted it and I did the same for them. I learned how to properly format a manuscript. I learned how to find markets and where to look for guidelines and how to follow them. I learned about science fiction conventions and why they were important to attend. I learned about other online spaces where SFF writers and readers and fans gathered. I learned what it meant to be a professional writer.

All that and I got tons of feedback on my stories and baby novel attempts from people who were smart and talented and went on to become pretty big deals.

I never would have gotten my first professional paying sale if not for the OWW. Never would have thought about Clarion or Clarion West and applied. Probably wouldn't have gotten in. That workshop made me a better writer right at a point in my life when I was in the best place to take advantage of what it had to offer.

The OWW doesn't exist in its original form, anymore. A few years after I joined, Del Rey stopped sponsoring it and the workshop went independent. It remained a great resource for me for many years after that. Then I went to Clarion West, and later I joined small writing groups online and in person, and at some point I left the OWW behind. It still exists (at sff.onlinewritingworkshop.com), as do many other online workshops with a similar model.

That magical combination of supportive community and in-depth feedback from writers with a wide range of skill and experience is hard, but not impossible, to find. If you haven't stumbled on it already, keep looking. The shape of it will change over time—much of what I benefited from in the OWW is now available in a dispersed way via social media—but the core vital elements remain the same. If you're at or near the beginning of your journey toward being a published writer, I encourage you to try and find a place where that combination exists online or in the place you live.

* * *

K. Tempest Bradford is a speculative fiction writer by night, a media critic and culture columnist by day, and an activist blogger in the interstices. Her fiction has appeared in award-winning magazines the likes of *Strange Horizons* and *Electric Velocipede* and bestselling anthologies *Diverse Energies*, *Federations*, *In the Shadow of the Towers*, plus many more. She's also a regular contributor to NPR, io9, and books about Time Lords. Visit her blog: KTempestBradford.com.

THE KEY TO THE KINGDOM, OR, HOW I SOLD *TOO LIKE THE LIGHTNING*

Ada Palmer

> Some people say revenge is living well –
> I've found it sometimes works to go away
> And *be more awesome*. Let him sit alone,
> To watch your wildfires leaping as you play.
>
> –Jo Walton, "Advice to Loki" 2013.

The midpoint first, then the primordial darkness, then the ever after.

It was 2011 (remember, this is the creation myth of a book that won't come out until 2016). I was in Florence, sitting in the top of a 13th century tower between Dante's house and my favorite gelato place (extra relevant in an un-air-conditioned August!), and talking to Jo Walton about whether or not I should start a blog. It was the beginning of a year in Florence, a postdoctoral research fellowship at the Villa I Tatti, Harvard's institute for Italian Renaissance studies. Life as a Renaissance historian had granted me long stays in Florence twice before, once on a student Fulbright, and once taking a shift as I Tatti's resident grad student mascot (#1 duty, be introduced to rich donors and look bright-eyed and promising). During my earlier stays I had written a series of emails describing my Italian experiences, and sent them to a list of friends and family. The list grew over time as the recipients recommended them to more distant cousins and acquaintances, until I had nearly a hundred people on my list. In fact, those emails were how I knew Jo. One of my roommates, Lila Garrott (herself a poet, author, book reviewer, and now editor at *Strange Horizons*), had posted a few of what, in neoclassical style, I called my "Ex Urbe" emails on her LiveJournal, where Jo had enjoyed them. In 2008 Jo had invited Lila and the rest of our eclectic household to visit her for Farthing Party in Montreal. Jo was with me in Italy that August because the question "Do you want to come stay in my apartment in a 13th century tower in Florence?" has one correct answer. "I wonder if it would be less work to just post them on a blog," I said, overwhelmed by trying to assemble the new list of people who had asked to receive my emails. Jo looked at me very seriously. "If you make a blog, I'll send the link to Patrick Nielsen Hayden."

I did make a blog.

In three months, it was in the sidebar of Making Light.

In six months, Patrick asked Jo if the author of this ExUrbe blog had written any fiction.

In two years (almost to the day, August 2013) Patrick bought *Too Like the Lightning*.

~o0o~

My appetite to see my fiction in print had been overwhelming since elementary school, and I vividly remember the thrill of standing on tiptoe to watch my first typed story (a single paragraph, about blue-and-silver alien raccoons) crawl its way out of the astounding new dot matrix printer at Dad's office. I had begun a novel by fourth grade, three by tenth, and I devoured summer writing courses, of which the courses on essay writing (Johns Hopkins) and prose poetry (Interlochen) proved far more valuable than the fiction ones. I remember once thinking to myself at fifteen, bored during a school convocation, that if I hadn't published a novel by twenty-five then…the end is vague. Then I should give up? Then I was a failure? Then I should curse the heavens? It was my first serious college writing mentor Hal Holiday who helped me understand how absurd that was. He made me cry in his office, with my first-ever B on a paper. I didn't understand what I'd done wrong. "Writing is a long apprenticeship," he said. I hadn't done anything wrong, but writing well—not well for your age group, but well in an absolute sense—was hard to achieve. It took real time. Spending every childhood summer and weekend writing, taking every summer writing course, those were good steps, they helped, but they were a beginning. I finished my first novel draft that year, flipped back to page one, and started writing it all over again.

In 2002, at twenty-one and with Mom to stuff the envelopes, I sent my (totally-rewritten) first novel-length manuscript winging its optimistic way to slush piles at agencies and publishers. I sometimes think, if we could harvest the emotional energy in all the fat manila query envelopes aspiring writers entrust to the post office every day, we could move planets. I have a folder of rejection letters from that first volley, and, looking over them now, I can see the good signs in them, the peppering of personalized notes, praise and encouragement among the form letters. I didn't understand then how many queries editors, agents and interns read, how generous it was for them to sacrifice precious seconds to write these extra lines (thank you!), but it did a lot to keep me going. And in the back of the folder I always kept a printout of Ursula Le Guin sharing a very grim rejection letter she received for *The Left Hand of Darkness*, with her note "This is included to cheer up anybody who just got a rejection letter. Hang in there!" Thank you. After eight months of agonizing suspense, and the sporadic gut-punch of rejections, that first volley got me an agent. She was not an F&SF specialist, but was game to try, and spent the next years doggedly marketing what neither of us realized was an unsalably long fantasy novel.

I don't remember where I received the wisdom that it's better to go on and write Book 1 of a new series rather than write Book 2 of a series when you haven't sold Book 1 yet. Wherever I got it from, I obeyed it, and soon my plucky agent was shopping two series, then three. Despite loving to sleep in, I followed the old advice and wrote in the morning, every day, an hour or two, giving my best hours to fiction and the rest of the day to the demands of grad school, and thereby wrote close to a million words of fiction over seven years. Looking over those practice projects now, I can see my writing improve with each, the sentences, the pace, the plot. Every paragraph was a step in that long apprenticeship. The wait stretched on—three years, four—and it hurt—the growing, gnawing appetite. Sometimes I would lie awake at night just from the pain of *wanting* something *so much*. But I had an agent, and that gave me confidence, and comfort.

Meanwhile I was working on my Ph.D. The single best thing that ever happened to my writing—looking at the novel I was working on at the time you can see the very chapter break where it happened, like lightning struck and *ZAP!* the prose was finally good—was in 2005, when I had to cut down my 20,000-word dissertation prospectus into a 7,000-word conference paper. Without knowing it, I had stumbled on "Half and Half Again," as it's called by people I know in journalism, a training exercise in which you go through the agony of cutting an old work down to half length, then half of that, learning to spot the chaff and bloat in your own work, and how to make it tight and powerful. Lightning. I published other things—my first academic article, blog pieces for Tokyopop about manga & cosplay, a Random Superpower Generator for Maple Leaf Games, but none of them eased the *wanting*. I also learned more about the world of genre publishing, from going to conventions and chatting with author friends made through Lila, and through my science fiction clubs, HRSFA (the Harvard-Radcliffe Science Fiction Society), and Double Star (at Bryn Mawr College). F&SF specialist agent

Donald Maass spoke to us at Vericon, a great little con HRSFA runs at Harvard every year, and I learned from his talk about the field, the extreme oversupply of submissions, the challenges of length and salability. I had queried Donald Maass (unsuccessfully) way back in 2002, but in 2006, with my writing much improved, preparing to begin a new series which I felt in my gut was leaps above the others (and eventually became the *Terra Ignota* series), I decided to break off my relationship with my first agent (with much gratitude and good will) and to try fresh to get a new agent at a major F&SF specialist agency.

I finished the first draft of *Too Like the Lightning* (Book 1 of *Terra Ignota*) in 2008, my penultimate year of graduate school. Between 2002 and 2008, plump manila envelopes had evolved into instantaneous e-queries, and my generic cover letters had acquired the varnish of name-dropping. I had recommendations from random people in the publishing world (Walter Isaacson, Priscilla Painton) whom I had met through Harvard. And, while my first 2002 volley had showered queries on dozens of doorsteps (many quite inappropriate), I sent *Too Like the Lightning* to only one press in 2008, my great hope: Tor. The more I learned about the world of genre publishing, the clearer it became that Tor was one of the few presses, if not the only one, that had the stability and resources to gamble on a big, fat science fiction series (four long books!) by a first time author, books which were dense and highbrow, and totally not similar to anything—trends are a safe investment; oddities are a gamble. Plus, I had an 'in'. There were people at Tor who were friends of friends, alumni and associates of both Bryn Mawr and Harvard, some of whom knew my Double Star and HRSFA connections. (Yes, I tried nepotism for all it was worth, anyone would—I still lay awake at nights, just *wanting*.)

After another year of lying awake and wanting (and finishing my Ph.D., and facing the academic job market, which in 2009 had just entered its sudden death spiral), a Tor contact told me (I think at Readercon?) that the book had advanced from the "slush" pile to the "shows promise" pile. This was good news, but an unagented manuscript, which the editor knows has been sent to no other press, can stew in that pile forever. That November I queried Donald Maass, hoping a kind word from Tor would help me get an agent, and that a good agent might prod along the literary glacier. I even got a Harvard-made mainstream publishing contact to email Donald Maass with his endorsement to accompany my query. (Roll for nepotism! Did it achieve anything? Not really!) On December 31st, I received an email from Donald apologizing for losing my query and getting back to me so late (apologizing for a delay of only two months! Such professionalism! Such sanity!) and saying he loved the beginning of the book, and was eager to read the whole thing. I sent it right away. I waited. I shopped other, older projects with a YA agent recommended by a friend (no luck). I published other things—more academic articles, critical essays, introductions to manga and anime releases. I stayed up nights. Sometimes it was so bad I couldn't go into a bookstore without feeling sick to my stomach. In November 2010 (a full year after Donald had asked for the book) Amy Boggs, then a fairly new member of the Donald Maass Agency, wrote to say that Donald—swamped by unspecified and mysterious *stuff*—had passed the book on to her, and she loved it. We finalized the contract by early December, and Amy started shopping the book around in the beginning of 2011.

~oOo~

That spring I received my I Tatti Fellowship, and that summer I sat in a tower in Florence with Jo Walton, contemplating a blog. Jo had talked to me about Patrick Nielsen Hayden, though I also knew of him from other sources; legends of such titans echo far through our little magic kingdom.

There is a fresco by Perugino in the Sistine Chapel, which shows St. Peter, in a beautiful neoclassical square, receiving the

Keys to Heaven from Christ, with a group of apostles and others gathered around to watch. It's a deeply tender moment, Peter's awe at the sight of the divinity who is also the friend he loves so much. But I can never see it without imagining the next panel of the comic book, where Christ has gone back to Heaven, and Peter is left in the square holding these enormous gold and silver keys, and everyone is standing around awkwardly, trying not to stare, and someone sidles up saying, "So...can I get you a cup of coffee?" You can't put them down, that's the thing, once you have the keys to Heaven, no one on Earth can forget it, not for an instant. And that's very much what it's like being an acquiring editor (I've described this to Patrick, he agrees), because you have the Keys to the Kingdom, and people around you—at conventions, at talks, online—want it *so much*. So much they lie awake at night. There are infinite horror stories about editors being harassed and chased at cons, having manuscripts shoved under bathroom stall doors, repeated emails which get weirder and more desperate. So, from childhood (picture me scrawny and eleven, following Dad and Uncle Bill to a Doctor Who convention, with my boy-short bright blonde hair, dressed as the Peter Davison Doctor) I had it drilled into me that you should never approach and bother an editor (or published author) about your manuscript. Q&A when they were on panels was okay, but outside that sphere, *verboten!* In fact, I had met Patrick at Farthing Party back in 2008, but, knowing who he was, I was an emotional wreck just being near him, racked between the Scylla of my desire and the Charybdis of the taboo, so I spent much of the weekend actively hiding around corners and behind pillars to avoid looking at him. But Jo knew I had a manuscript, and passed it on to Patrick for me in spring of 2012 when he asked her if the author of ExUrbe had written any fiction.

And I waited. And I lay awake at night. On a trip to New Orleans, an editor friend of Jo's told a story about a query which had taken twelve years to be accepted, which actually made me throw up. I tried to start another novel series, but I couldn't. *Terra*

Ignota meant too much to me, so I broke my own law and wrote Book 2. And Book 3. So many heartfelt eggs in that basket. Amy had occasional non-news for me, and I was overseeing the publication of my first nonfiction book, the academic history *Reading Lucretius in the Renaissance,* which will hopefully (knock all the wood you can!) get me tenure here at the magnificent I-dare-you-to-prove-it's-not-Hogwarts University of Chicago. (Where I teach history of magic. Really.) I had submitted the monograph proposal to Harvard University Press way back in 2009. Given the infamous snail's pace of academic publishing, I often thought of *Reading Lucretius in the Renaissance* and *Too Like the Lightning* as twins fighting to see which would be the first to make it out. But Tor, wonderful, infuriating, experimental, ambitious, field-shaping Tor, is slower.

In March 2013, Jo reported to me that Patrick had said positive things to her about the first page of *Too Like the Lightning.* One page down, 333 to go. That spring and summer were the madness of producing and recording my two-hour close harmony a cappella Viking stage musical *Sundown: Whispers of Ragnarok*, and its demands were exhaustion enough to let me mostly sleep. As August came along, Patrick told Jo to tell me (in our surrealist game of telephone) that he and Teresa wanted to have dinner with me at Worldcon in San Antonio, and I should have my answer then. This was more than a year after Patrick had asked for the manuscript, and five years after I had first submitted it to Tor.

I was working a booth at that Worldcon, an outreach display for the Texas A&M University Cushing Memorial Library and Archives, which has one of the world's great science fiction collections, an impregnable treasure vault full of rare pulps, fanzines, first editions, and the archived papers of authors from Star Trek scriptwriters, to George R.R. Martin, to (now) me. (Are you a writer? Do you have random papers and notes from old projects cluttering your house? Cushing's awesome librarians totally want to take your clutter, index it, and preserve it for posterity! Win-win!) The first morning of Worldcon, I was walking through the dealers' room on my way to our booth, when Jo Walton gestured me over to the table where she was doing a signing. I gestured back that I didn't want to interrupt the people who were waiting patiently in line, but she flailed emphatically, so I came. She told me that Patrick told her to tell me "Yes." I remember hugging, and crying, and intense crying, and gasping out a vague apology to the guy who was in the front of the line, but he said "It's okay, it's clearly important." Jo smiled at him and said, "She's just sold her first novel!" A keen, satisfied brightness entered his face, like when you taste an unexpectedly excellent sour candy, and he said, "So, it does happen."

Most of the rest of the San Antonio Worldcon is lost in the mists of bliss amnesia. I remember staggering back to the Cushing booth all puffy and red-faced, and struggling to communicate to my colleague Todd Samuelson that I was okay, just overhappy from yes! Yes! YES! I remember I couldn't find my phone to text my dear friend Carl Engle-Laird (an HRSFA alum, who was then a new editorial assistant at Tor.com, and sharing my suspense) so I borrowed a phone from Lauren Schiller (my singing partner and roommate of 10+ years), only I couldn't see through my tears, so the message came out all garbled and full of typos and r5and0m nuMB4rs. I was on a panel right after that, with Lila Garrott (whose online connections had been so instrumental in all this), and I had no time to tell her before the panel, so I just typed it on my then-recovered cell phone and set it on the table in front of us: "Patrick said yes." She glowed.

After Jo's signing, we found Patrick in the concessions area, and there ensued perhaps the most absurd conversation I shall ever have. I was still paralyzed by the aftereffects of Scylla and Charybdis, so shy and overwhelmed that I could barely force myself to look directly at the legendary Patrick. But Patrick is himself a naturally shy person, and skittish after so many years carrying the Keys to Heaven, so he couldn't look at me either. And there we were, both trying to hide behind Jo (who is a head shorter than both of us), unable to make eye contact while trying to talk about how we wanted to work together for the rest of our careers. That was when I started to see the absurd flip side of it: all the while that I had been terrified of approaching this incredibly important editor who had power over everything I ever wanted, in his world I had been the intimidating one, this distant Harvard Ph.D., with all these impressive publications, this learned and authoritative tone on my blog, and *I* had everything *he* wanted, great science fiction that it would be a pleasure to publish. In Settlers of Catan terms, I had bricks, he had wood, but we were so mutually overwhelmed neither of us could get the words out: "Shall we make this road?" We had dinner with Jo and Teresa at one of those Brazilian barbecue places, where they hunt the great beasts of the plains and serve them to you on spits carried by excessively statuesque young men—at least that's what Jo says, because bliss amnesia has erased everything except a vague memory of asparagus and a beige tablecloth. I remember Patrick said he and Teresa wanted to audition to edit and shape my career. Audition? I would have begged!

Patrick took me to the Tor party that weekend. I know he introduced me to Tom Doherty and fifty other genre VIPs, but I genuinely don't remember a thing except recognizing Liz Gorinsky from a distance by her hair. Patrick forgot to give me his business card, so I almost left without the ability to contact him. It took three weeks to stop feeling like a dream. No, that's not true—it still feels like a dream. I signed the four-book contract by crackling firelight, huddling over the hearthstone during the power outage caused by a New Year's blizzard, which absolutely feels like a dream. I have a release date now (that took two years), and cover art (same), and the Advanced Bound Manuscript in front of me (well, a defective ABM missing the last three chapters—oops!), and I have a fantastic recording of Patrick—*the* Patrick—playing guitar with me while I sing my ode to fandom's support of space exploration "Somebody Will" (super ultra win condition!). But I still feel prepared to wake up tomorrow, back in my old bedroom, and discover it was all a dream. Maybe there will always be that edge of doubt, the scar of how intensely I worried that the door might never open. Sometimes it doesn't. But if it did open for me, it wasn't because I kept pounding on the gate with the same desperate query. And it wasn't the favor-trading, or the Harvard connections, or my attempts at nepotism, or even (honestly) my agent (though she's done so many great things for me then and since). It was that I set forth to be more awesome. I kept honing my craft, starting new projects better than the last, producing other works, articles, music, essays, research, the blog. I made my fire burn bright in the dark. People do see.

* * *

Ada Palmer's first science fiction novel *Too Like the Lightning* (volume one of *Terra Ignota*, from Tor Books) explores how humanity's cultural and historical legacies might evolve in a future of borderless nations and globally commixing populations. She teaches in the University of Chicago History Department, studying the Renaissance, Enlightenment, classical reception, the history of books, publication and reading, and the history of philosophy, heresy, science and atheism, and is the author of *Reading Lucretius in the Renaissance* (Harvard University Press). She often researches in Italy, usually in Florence or at the Vatican. She composes fantasy, SF and mythology-themed music, including the Viking mythology musical stage play *Sundown: Whispers of Ragnarok* (available on CD and DVD), and often performs at conventions with her vocal group Sassafrass. She also researches anime/manga, especially Osamu Tezuka, early post-WWII manga and gender in manga, and has worked as a consultant for many anime and manga publishers. She blogs for Tor.com, and writes the philosophy & travel blog ExUrbe.com. Her website is www.adapalmer.com.

MY PATH TO PUBLICATION, AND MY OTHER PATH TO PUBLICATION

Ken Scholes

The question comes up all the time—in interviews, in the Q&A at book signings, at conventions—and I remember asking the question myself back when I was eager to nose my career onto Publication Highway:

"How did you become a published author?" (Redundancy intended.)

It's actually a good question—I think we can learn a lot from other writers' approaches to business and craft and it can encourage us when that latest rejection comes across the email. So I'm absolutely happy to answer it.

For me, it feels very much like there are two answers. I'm going to give you the one everyone gets excited about and then I'm going to give you the other.

Back in 2005, two big things happened in my writing career. I won the Writers of the Future contest with my Hodgson/Houdini mash-up, "Into the Blank Where Life is Hurled," and I wrote a little (I thought) throw-away one-off about a mechanical oddity and the king who found him, "Of Metal Men and Scarlet Thread and Dancing with the Sunrise." That first story was my first publication at professional level (based on the SFWA guidelines at the time) and the second became my second, shortly after winning the award.

That next year, my short stories started showing up in more and more pro-level markets along with a healthy smattering of semi-pro or small-press markets. And my friends (and even a few editors) started asking me about novels. It took a while, but eventually my pal Jay (Lake) and my partner Jen took me to dinner and dared me to just do it. I expanded that story about the metal man, Isaak, into my very first novel and then some—the opening salvo in a five-volume saga.

I started the book on September 11, 2006 and finished it October 27, 2006. I wrote fast in every nook and cranny I could find in my life (on Jay's advice). Jay and Jen dared me, and Jay's end of the deal was that if I had a finished draft of *Lamentation* by the end of October, he would introduce me to everyone he'd met while marketing *Mainspring* (and Jay, as you know, knew *everyone*). So I wrote the book, convinced it was crap. If it had been up to me, I'd have quit at chapter 5.

And here's the thing: Jay loved the book. And then so did everyone else who read it in those early stages. The following week, at World Fantasy in Austin, Jay's agent—Jennifer Jackson—asked me to send it to her when revisions were complete. I sent it over in January, and she took me on as a client in February.

That spring, I met Beth Meacham (Jay's editor at Tor) while at Norwescon. She had heard about *Lamentation,* and though we'd met in passing at a few cons, this time we sat down and started getting to know each other. I thought she and Tor were a perfect fit for my series, and in mid-October of 2007, while home with the flu, I got that phone call where your agent asks you if you're sitting down. "I can be," I said as I sat. And then Jenn Jackson told me that Tor wanted all five books for what was a wildly good deal for a first-time novelist. The book came out in 2009, picked up some awards and some rave reviews, and launched me nicely further into my writing career. Now, here in 2016, I'm working on the fifth book of that first contract and staring at nearly a decade spent mostly in the Named Lands with Rudolfo, Isaak and the gang.

At the time, folks were talking about the awesomeness of my overnight success. From starting the draft of your first novel to landing a five-book contract in just over a year. Pretty cool, yeah?

Of course, that's the story everyone likes to hear. And it's true. But it's true like the tip of the iceberg is truly the iceberg. There's more beneath the surface than what you can see. And this path actually is rather usual and common and less exciting.

You see, I wrote a novel that ended up being publishable. But before I wrote it, I wrote a lot of short stories. And before I did that (and while doing it), I read a lot. And soaked my soul in story for a lifetime before that first novel and the sudden rise of my star in the world of books.

At fourteenish, I read Bradbury's essay, "How to Keep and Feed a Muse," and it caught me on fire. I wrote to him and he told me to write a thousand words a day until I had my million bad words. So I was writing stories out by hand before I learned to type (yes, on a typewriter) and then, like Bradbury and countless others, I threw those short stories into the mail and kept hoping something would stick. Then at seventeen I set it aside for a decade. When I came back to it, post-college, I jammed out more stories (now on a PC) and after over twenty short stories and around seventy-five rejections, I landed that first sale to a semi-pro magazine, *Talebones*. A year later, I sold another after more rejections. And a year later, I sold my first really popular story (also to *Talebones*) and that story ("Edward Bear and the Very Long Walk") led to my friendship with Jay.

By the time I won Writers of the Future, I'd sold maybe a dozen stories to the small presses that were under the radar because of their size and pay scale. I built (and sold) a lot of short stories before I tackled that first novel, and I built a lot of relationships in the business before I went out trying to find an agent and publisher for it. And I let other people who happened to love my work promote me. And I got on with writing the next book.

There are a lot of publication stories that on the surface look pretty unusual and exciting, but scratch the surface and a lot of them come back to writing a lot in the face of rejection over time—and submitting those words for an editor to accept or reject—like most skills that require regular practice.

So stay the course. If a Trailer Boy like me can pull it off, then I suspect you can too. If you don't give up.

* * *

Ken Scholes is the award-winning, critically-acclaimed author of four novels and over forty-five short stories. His work has appeared in print for over fifteen years.

Ken's eclectic background includes time spent as a label gun repairman, a sailor who never sailed, a soldier who commanded a desk, a preacher (he got better), a nonprofit executive, a musician and a government procurement analyst before settling into writing and raising twin daughters for a living. He has a degree in History from Western Washington University.

Ken is a native of the Pacific Northwest and makes his home in Saint Helens, Oregon. You can learn more about Ken by visiting www.kenscholes.com.

THE MEANDERING PATH

Nancy Jane Moore

A long time ago (though not in a galaxy far, far away), I took a weekend-long writing class from Marion Zimmer Bradley at the Omega Institute. I'd been writing for a while—like most writers I know, I'd been playing around with writing since childhood—but I hadn't figured out how to get serious about it.

In those days, the Omega Institute—a kind of new-age summer camp for grown-ups—was my go-to vacation, the place where I went to relax and escape. The workshop with Marion didn't fit their usual mold, but it caught my eye. I was trying to write adventure stories with female protagonists and I'd read some of the Sword and Sorceress series she edited.

It was a large class, and given the time constraints, she couldn't read a whole story from each of us, so she had us write the beginning of a story. My story began, "She had just enough time to scream 'Retreat' to her troops before the impact of the arrow hitting her chest knocked her to the ground."

Marion critiqued the intros in the next session and she said positive things about mine. So I went home from Omega, finished the story, and sent it to her for Sword and Sorceress. It was the first piece of fiction I felt confident enough about to submit and, in fact, the first short story I'd written that worked as a story by itself instead of sounding like a piece of a novel.

She bought it. Which is to say, I sold the first decent short story I ever wrote to the first market I sent it to. I joined SFWA as an associate member and figured my career was set.

I also started taking classes at the Writer's Center in Bethesda, Maryland, met other science fiction and fantasy writers, and ended up in a good writers' group. The next year I sold Marion a flash fiction for the next volume of *Sword and Sorceress*.

And then I didn't sell another damn story for about six years. That wasn't even a real sale—I won a contest sponsored by the *National Law Journal* with a legal-themed science fiction story. That gave me the confidence to apply to Clarion West, which turned out to be one of the best experiences of my adult life. When I got a call out of the blue the next year offering to buy film rights for the story in the *Law Journal*, I thought I was set again.

I did sell short fiction consistently after that, but I didn't become a big name or make enough money to quit my day job. Or even enough money to remotely consider quitting my day job. In fact, I went full time as a legal editor and reporter after I came back from Clarion West. While I didn't find enough satisfaction in that kind of writing to quit doing fiction, I did learn a lot about writing good sentences and making things clear to different audiences.

I had a couple of books published (a novella and a collection), sold a lot of short stories and a fair number of essays, and joined Book View Café. Finally in 2015 Aqueduct Press published my first novel. It's had some nice reviews and I even got a royalty check at the end of December.

I've given up on thinking I'm set, though. The only thing that's "set" at this point is that I'm going to keep writing exactly what I want to write and figure that sooner or later I'll find a home for it. That's probably not the financially prudent way to run a writing career, but it makes me happy. These days, that's good enough.

* * *

Nancy Jane Moore is the author of *The Weave*, a science fiction novel published in 2015 by Aqueduct Press, several other books, and numerous short stories. She belongs to SFWA and is a founding member of the authors' co-op Book View Café. Every Thursday she blogs at http://bookviewcafe.com/blog/. She lives in Oakland, CA. http://nancyjanemoore.com/.

NO ONE TRUE WAY

Jennifer Brozek

I've found many different paths to publication and none of them involved an agent. In fact, I am certain there is no "standard" way to get published. Especially in this day and age of conventions and the internet.

~o0o~

My first fiction collection, *In a Gilded Light: 105 Tales of the Macabre*, was a complete accident. I needed to teach myself how to write short, concise fiction. So, I started writing what I called my "Freaky Friday Fictions." Every Friday, I would take something that happened to me in the previous week and I would turn it into a piece of flash fiction less than 1,000 words long. Almost every story had a supernatural bent to it.

I broke every social rule of writing. I killed off friends and family and co-workers. I had so much fun with it that my friends started asking me to be murdered...or to be the murderer in my *Freaky Friday Fiction* pieces. I was happy to oblige. After about two and a half years, I announced that I was done with the writing exercise and that *Freaky Friday Fictions* was no more.

Much to my surprise, two small press publishing houses contacted me and asked if they could publish the collection. They were never meant to be published professionally. In the end, the collection was sold to Dark Quest Books and has continued to be a good seller.

~oOo~

My first anthology, *Grants Pass*, took me five years to sell. I pitched it to publishers, agents, and editors. I talked to people at conventions and got nowhere. Though, most encouraged me to keep trying. I ended up asking one of the authors I already had a story from who owned a small press, Morrigan Books, if he'd be interested in the book. He was. He withdrew his story, assigned me a co-editor, Amanda Pillar, and had me trash half the stories I'd originally accepted. I learned a lot with that one. Also I won my first publishing award.

My second anthology, *Close Encounters of the Urban Kind*, was an accidental sale. I mentioned to Jason Sizemore of Apex Publications that I'd like to do an anthology of urban legends based on alien encounters. He asked me a bunch of questions. I just thought we were talking. A week later he told me, "Okay, I'm going to buy your anthology." I was confused, then stunned. I hadn't known I was selling him on the anthology.

~oOo~

I sold my first pro, tie-in story to John Helfers while having a conversation with him at a convention. I'd written for him before for RPGs. He knew I could write. I knew he edited the *Valdemar* anthologies with Mercedes Lackey. I think I said something along the lines of "I'd love to write a bardic story for one of those." His enthusiastic response got me an invite to the anthology. I was accepted in on the strength of my pitch. The story was bought on the strength of the writing and plot.

~oOo~

As for how I got started writing for role-playing games—the thing that launched my career—I played in a text-based MUCK (Multi-User Created Kingdom) with Sean Everette. I played a bard who told original stories in character. He knew I reviewed RPGs for *Black Gate* magazine. He asked me to do reviews for him for *Campaign* magazine. When Sean was hired by Sovereign Stone as an editor, he immediately hired me to write for him on two Dragonlance supplements: *Holy Order of Stars* and *Time of the Twins*. He knew I could write to word count and deadline.

~o0o~

In all cases, while I had some professional work to back me up, each one of these editors and publishers took a chance on me. I was at the right place at the right time. I said the right thing and wrote the right words. I'm still selling through unconventional means today: recommended to publishers through other authors, being approached at conventions and asked to pitch a story, being contacted online and asked if I was open to contracts.

There are so many different paths to publication that I know I'm going to keep finding new ones as my career progresses. Maybe, someday, I'll even go down a more traditional path with an agent.

* * *

Jennifer Brozek is a Hugo Award-nominated editor and an award-winning author. She has worked in the publishing industry since 2004. With the number of edited anthologies, novel sales, RPG books, and nonfiction books under her belt, Jennifer is often considered a Renaissance woman, but she prefers to be known as a wordslinger and optimist. Read more about her at www.jenniferbrozek.com or follow her on Twitter: @JenniferBrozek.

TIMELINE KEY POINTS

Rhiannon Held

When asked how I got my first traditional publishing contract, I often try to minimize the story, because through superhuman luck, I skipped out on a whole big wad of the typical waiting. Then, I didn't want to make anyone stuck in their own waiting period feel more despair by comparison. Now, I've entered into a waiting period of my own with one series dropped and another on my editor's desk, as yet unread. I *especially* don't want to dwell on the one-time-only nature of that early luck now.

Instead, I've discovered it helps to look back on the path to my first contract as a series of key points in a time traveling story. The kind of points that seem like, when changed, they should send the timeline careening off into a terrible alternate universe wherein Nazis rule the world. And yet—twist!—the timeline adjusts and the order of the universe is maintained as a new event leads to the same result. Maybe at a different time, maybe at a different place, but the same result nonetheless. I fully believe that's true of my writing career—if *this* hadn't happened, or I'd missed *that* opportunity, I would still be an author now. At a different time, in a different place, but still an author. It's a belief that keeps me going through the waiting. If not *this* editor, another. If not *that* series, the one after it.

What I think of as the first key point in my career as a novelist came during the grueling—and amazing—learning experience that is the six-week, Clarion-style Odyssey Writing Workshop. At that time, I was writing exclusively short fiction. In a private conversation with the director, Jeanne Cavelos, I asked if I should maybe push myself into writing a novel, though I was one semester away from graduating with my master's degree, and would be hip-deep in my thesis when I left the workshop. She told me, "Don't write a novel until you can't *not* write a novel."

The next year, I submitted one of my short stories to the Norwescon Writers' Workshop, and was paired with Beth Meacham, who eventually became my editor. She was impressed with my story and gave me the proverbial business card—if I ever wrote a novel, she told me I should send it to her. I was new enough to the world of professional writing at the time that I didn't understand the magnitude of the opportunity I'd been offered. Perhaps that was for the best, because I wrote a novel when I was ready, not when I thought I should to take advantage of an opportunity that was, as promised, not time limited. At the time I was handed the card, I had my M.A. and a job offer, but a relocation to another city across the state still to come. Novels were the last thing on my mind.

Three years later came a third key point. I'd been role-playing online for years, and the game was as filled with drama as pretty much any internet club is, composed as it was of human beings with all their tendencies to gossip, take sides, and say accidentally—or sometimes intentionally—hurtful things to each other. I was involved in a blow-up—with fault on both sides, viewed with hindsight—which left me hurting and questioning a few friendships. I realized I needed to escape from the situation to get distance and perspective, so I decided that was the time I couldn't *not* write a novel. I picked a short story my critique group had said was ripe for being expanded, and dived in.

I credit my fourth key point to John Pitts, who writes as J.A. Pitts. I'd had two, three rounds of critique on that novel, revising between each, but there were always more improvements to be made. We were on the same flight back from World Fantasy that year, and ending up chatting in the airport, wrapped in the fuzz of post-con exhaustion. He knew about Beth giving me her card, and asked when I was going to send her my novel. "I have more revising to do," I told him. "I still haven't addressed the last set of comments. There are several things I completely agree need to be fixed, so I won't be happy until I fix them."

"That's fine," he said. "But after that, you send it." I probably protested more, I don't remember precisely, but he stuck to his assertion. I needed to send it. So after one more revision, I dug out Beth's card from my travel bag where it had rested safely for three years to get her email, and sent the novel.

Beth read my novel astoundingly quickly, compared to the publishing industry's usual pace, made me an offer, and I was suddenly scrambling to contact agents. I found one who was a good fit and excited to take me on, Cameron McClure, and the rest—as they say—was my first traditional publishing contract.

That would make a good high note for an ending, but as I noted in at the beginning of this essay, I've unfortunately lived past that point. The three books I was contracted for sold decently, but not well enough for my publisher to want a fourth, and there was nothing my editor could do about it. I've finished the first book in a new series and I'm working with my agent to get it sold, but meanwhile, I wait.

And believe that whatever points future events turn on, my timeline will find its way to where it's meant to go.

* * *

Rhiannon Held is the author of the Silver series of urban fantasy novels. She lives in Seattle, where she works as an archaeologist for an environmental compliance firm. Working in both archaeology and writing, she's "lucky" enough to have two sexy careers that don't make her much money. In her proverbial copious free time, she still games online, sings in a community choir, and occasionally enjoys betting on the ponies. Find her online at rhi-annonheld.com and on Twitter as @rhiannonheld.

NOT DELUDED: HOW I SOLD
MY FIRST NOVEL

Jo Walton

When I sold my first novel, it made sense of my whole life.

It was 1998, when dinosaurs roamed the earth. I was thirty-three, the age Jesus was crucified and Dante went into the dark wood. I was six years older than Keats was when he died. I was at an age when it's easy to fall into the trap of believing that if you haven't started to achieve something you never will. Right up to the part where I sold the novel my life looked like a mess. I had a resume that was just a list of inconsequential jobs, though all stuff you do sitting down, because I have a lame leg that makes it painful for me to stand. I was receiving a benefit Britain had at that time which gave you money to make up your earnings to the amount you would have been given if you were on welfare. I had a seven-year-old son. The year before I had ended my first marriage over my need to take my writing seriously. What I didn't have was any evidence my writing was worth taking seriously, worth shaping my life around. I had done it anyway. But I had done it as a pure act of faith. I had published nothing but a bunch of roleplaying stuff—and writing gaming things can be the kiss of death to being taken seriously as a fiction writer.

There was no difference between me at that point and

somebody who was a deluded failure. I was writing every day between about 5 a.m. and precisely 8 a.m., when my son got up. (All of my first three books were written before 8 a.m.) But I had already run across people who talked seriously about their writing but whose work was terrible. At bad moments in the middle of the night I was convinced I was just like them. What was more likely, after all?

Worst of all, not only did I worry that I might be insane to believe my writing mattered, I also worried that I couldn't possibly be a real writer. I had stopped writing and started again. When I was twenty-two, my first husband had read what I was writing and told me it was awful, and I believed him and stopped. Then, eventually, about seven years later, I started again. People say real writers keep on writing, but since I've been successful I've always been very open about this stopping and starting. The myth of writers not being able to stop is very pervasive. I want other writers to understand that it can be okay. After I started writing again, after years of writing nothing but editorials, reviews, roleplaying stuff, and conversational usenet posts, I'd improved out of all recognition. But as of 1998 this was just in my own opinion, and that of a couple of online friends. Most of my friends didn't even know I was writing a novel—I didn't talk about it, after all, what was the point? I didn't have any solid external validation of the value of my work, or my sanity. And wasn't I getting a little old to be a starving artist in a garret?

So I was a middle-aged disabled single mother with no money and no achievements, but I was happy. I spent a lot of time on usenet, talking about writing and books with people all over the world. Usenet was a stegosaur-powered topic-based collection of newsgroups, where people gathered to talk. Somehow there were just the right number of people for this to work, and many of them were awesome. On usenet I found people who would take me seriously. For the first time I had a community who paid attention to what I had to say about things I cared about. The joke was that nobody could tell you were a dog—on the internet nobody could tell I was somebody's mom with three part-time jobs. I was somebody with opinions that people respected. My usenet friends were all over the world and none of them were local to me, but at good moments that made it all the more science-fictional and niftier.

I completed a novel called *The Rebirth of Pan* in 1997, my first novel after I started writing again. I printed it out and sent it, at vast expense, with a whole raft of International Reply Coupons, across the Atlantic to Patrick Nielsen Hayden at Tor, then as now, the best SF publisher on the planet.

I remember going home from the post office, full of hope and fear. Sending off a novel to an editor has the emotional weight of a combination of a job application and a proposal of marriage—and then after you send it you wait, and wait, and wait for a response, heart in mouth.

I sent it to Patrick and not to a UK publisher partly because I'd run into Patrick on usenet, and so at least he knew who I was. (Also, although I didn't know it, he'd read my poetry, which I'd put online in hand-carved HTML—I didn't have a browser so I had to go to the library to check if my links worked.) Patrick had published Maureen McHugh's brilliant *China Mountain Zhang,* and we liked a lot of the same books. It seemed possible he might like what I was writing. But mostly, I felt that in sending it to Tor I had at least a chance. Sending it to a UK publisher in 1998 would have been pointless. One of my part-time jobs had been working in an SF bookshop. I knew what was being published in the UK, and it didn't look anything like what I was writing. If you weren't ironic, you couldn't possibly be taken seriously. It was a great time to get things published if they were sly, cynical, cool. I wasn't any of those things. I was full of passionate intensity about everything all the time. Also the US market seemed more open to publishing women. I was right about this. Even with success in the US and an agent, I couldn't get published in the UK until 2012.

Months after I sent off the novel, Patrick sent me email. In those dial-up days, on my old 286, email announced itself and then slowly downloaded. I can still remember the mixture of excitement and dread in my gut as the hard drive whirred. And the email—as Ada Palmer said in her piece for this book, editors hold the Keys to the Kingdom, and they can't ever put them down. The email was to say Patrick was going to be at a fan gathering in London and asking if I was going to be there. Not a word about the book. Just a human being, wanting to hang out. Okay. But it's very hard for a writer and an editor not to have those huge keys get in the way. I couldn't help building castles in the air. I went to London for the meetup, at some considerable effort of arranging babysitting, and much uncomfortable juggling of finances. Patrick was indeed there, and not only did he not say a word to me about the book, he didn't say a word to me about anything. He is shy. I am not shy. But I wanted to be published so much that I couldn't possibly talk about it, and couldn't walk up to him and start talking about anything else either. It wasn't just that I wanted to sell a book and validate my life and all my choices. Much more than that, I wanted to sell a book to become part of the conversation of science fiction.

I went home on the train. I was almost at the end of writing the first volume of *The King's Peace*. I stared out of the window at the grey, rainy, unrelieved misery of Slough ("Come friendly bombs...") and refused to cry. I bit my lip and shut away all the disappointment, all the aching, and the fact that there is insanity in my family, and forced myself think about my characters. After all, they had it much worse than I did. I went home and got on with writing.

In March 1998, Patrick emailed me again. My mailbox was so full at that point that it took about ten minutes to download and open, and I went and cleaned the bathroom while my 286 whirred because I couldn't take the suspense. After all that, it was a rejection. But it was the best possible rejection. Patrick said *The Rebirth of Pan* wasn't publishable as it was, but it was the kind of thing people wrote who were going to write really good things later. He said it wasn't a good idea to try doctoring it into publication, that I should write something else and send it to him. Well, *The King's Peace* was done and I was writing volume two. I replied instantly and said I had another novel I'd finished while I'd been waiting, and might he like to see it in email? I went online again right away to send the reply the same day, something I almost never did because it was dial-up and I paid by the minute. When I got back to the computer after reading my son his bedtime story, Patrick had agreed, asking for the first three chapters. I could hardly see the screen as I attached and sent them. Two days later, he asked for the rest of it.

Then I waited again. Compared to how long some people have waited it was nothing, March to July. But every day of it felt like forever.

In July 1998 my son was in Lancaster staying with his dad for a week and I was in Ireland visiting Emmet, now my second husband. I'd met him on usenet. He was finishing up his Bioinformatics PhD at the University of Cork. I didn't have a laptop, and he didn't either—it's almost unimaginable now how we thought we were so wired, practically cyborgs, living in the future of what we'd grown up in, me with my dial-up and my beloved 286, him with internet only at work, neither of us with phones. He didn't even have a landline. I could be out of communication for days at a time. This kind of thing was normal, in those primitive times. (It wasn't that long ago! How did this become something I have to explain, like something from a historical novel?)

Meanwhile, Patrick was in New York, and the day had come when he'd read the rest of *The King's Peace*, and he wanted to buy it, right now, at light speed, no, faster than that. He sent me email. I was in Ireland, and didn't see it. He waited—minutes, hours, all day. Editors aren't used to waiting. He asked on usenet if anyone knew where I was. A friend in Canada emailed him Emmet's email address. Emmet went to work, read his email, found out that Patrick wanted to buy my book, abandoned his desk and ran home across the city (dodging velociraptors…) to tell me. He was thrilled and proud. I almost fainted. Patrick had said he wanted to telephone me to discuss it. I went back to the office with Emmet. He emailed Patrick and we arranged a time for Patrick to call me, necessarily in Emmet's office. While I took the call, we made Emmet's co-workers wait out on the stairs with the baby brontosaurs.

Patrick bought my book, and it felt like a dream. I was delighted and relieved but I kept thinking I was going to wake up. I went back to Britain and took a train up to Lancaster to collect my son. In the bright sunshine, moving through the lovely stone-walled north country, I gave Lake District travel advice to a very nice American couple. Making conversation, they asked me what I did. The words "I've just sold my first novel" came out of my mouth. That's when it felt real, and felt like a total vindication of my whole life.

My son wasn't even a tiny bit excited by my big news. "That's why you were writing it," he said. He had believed in me axiomatically. If I'd been deluded, I'd have let him down too.

After that, well, it was two and a half years to publication, which felt endless. All kinds of things happened—I got an agent and a contract. Tom Doherty read it and liked it and thought it could be successful as a fat fantasy novel, so we changed the contract and Tor ended up publishing what I thought of as all volumes one and two together, and then volume three separately. I had one of the worst copyedits of all time—Patrick rang me TransAtlantic to apologise for how bad was. The book came out in the US and of course I was still in the UK. To make it worse, there was a postal strike so I didn't get to see any actual copies for weeks. Patrick posted on usenet on the day it came out to say how proud he was, and a jerk said he couldn't tell the difference between that and advertising and turned the thread that should have been a celebration into a flame war.

But the book was out, and people were reading it—just a few people at first. It was real and out there and part of the conversation, as I'd always wanted. I was nominated for the Campbell Award, and Emmet and I got married and went to the MilPhil Worldcon as a honeymoon. There I got to see the book on actual shelves, and had the best time losing the award.

Then the second book came out, and we moved to Canada. I was nominated again but couldn't afford to go to San Jose for Worldcon, but won the Campbell. I wrote more books, won the World Fantasy Award, was nominated for a Nebula, won the Prometheus Award, and the Mythopoeic Award. I wrote eight novels, and was making more money writing than I had been before, and anyway, Canada has a much lower cost of living, and Emmet had a job. Then I wrote *Among Others* and it was a surprise success and won a Nebula and a Hugo and was published in sixteen languages and even in the UK. Lots of people really loved it. Since 2011, I have really been making enough money to live on. Now it's thirteen novels and a Locus Award-winning collection of essays, and the level of demi-fame that there's a reasonable chance if you read in genre that you vaguely know who I am. And since 2000, more and more people have been reading my books, talking about them, comparing other books to them, being influenced by them, loving them, hating them, responding to them, thinking things they wouldn't have thought without them. And I no longer wake in the night thinking I may be insane to believe in the value of my writing, or feeling that my life is a purposeless mess.

"Cattle die, kinsmen die, the gods themselves will one day die, only wordfame dies not, for one who well achieves it." And since that's Odin speaking, there's a typically sneaky qualification on that last bit, because nobody ever does achieve wordfame well enough that it won't eventually die. Books are published and talked about and in time forgotten. But it's enough. My books exist now and are part of the ongoing conversation. My best work is always still to come.

* * *

Editor's Note: When I asked the authors for their bios, Jo told me she had two, and one was a poem; which one did I want? I told her to send them both, and I would choose. Well, they're both delightful and informative, and editors get to make their own rules about such things, so here they both are.

Jo Walton has published twelve novels, with a thirteenth, *Necessity*, out this summer. She has also published three poetry collections and an essay collection. She won the John W. Campbell Award for Best New Writer in 2002, the World Fantasy Award for *Tooth and Claw* in 2004, the Hugo and Nebula awards for *Among Others* in 2012, and in 2014 both the Tiptree Award for *My Real Children* and the Locus Non Fiction award for *What Makes This Book So Great*. She comes from Wales but lives in Montreal where the food and books are much better. She gets bored easily so she tends to write books that are different from each other. She also reads a lot, enjoys travel, talking about books, and eating great food. She plans to live to be ninety-nine and write a book every year. Her website is www.jowaltonbooks.com.

Jo Walton
has run out of eggs and needs to go buy some,
she has no time to write a bio
as she wants to make spanakopita today.
She also wants to write a new chapter
and fix the last one.
Oh yes, she writes stuff,
when people leave her alone to get on with it
and don't demand bios
and proofreading and interviews
and dinner.

Despite constant interruptions
she has published nine novels
in the last forty-eight years
and started lots of others.
She won the Campbell for Best New Writer in 2002
when she was 38.
She has also written half a ton of poetry
which isn't surprising as she finds poetry
considerably easier to write
than short bios listing her accomplishments.
She is married, with one (grown up, awesome) son
who lives nearby with his girlfriend and two cats.
She also has lots of friends
who live all over the planet
who she doesn't see often enough.
She remains confused by punctuation,
"who" and "whom"
and "that" and "which".
She cannot sing and has trouble with arithmetic
also, despite living ten years in Montreal
her French still sucks.
Nevertheless her novel *Among Others*
won a Hugo and a Nebula
so she must be doing something right
at least way back when she wrote it
it'll probably never work again.
She also won a World Fantasy Award in 2004
for an odd book called *Tooth and Claw*
in which everyone is dragons.
She comes from South Wales
and identifies ethnically
as a Romano-Briton
but she emigrated to Canada
because it seemed a better place
to stand to build the future.

She blogs about old books on Tor.com
and posts poetry and recipes and wordcount on her LJ
and is trying to find something to bribe herself with
as a reward for writing a bio
that isn't chocolate.

April 2013

Update, February 2016
Since then she has written another four novels,
and published a collection of blog posts
and her son has broken up with his girlfriend
though they're still good friends.
She knows it's a cliché, but tonight's dinner will be stew,
followed by blackcurrant crumble,
because she has run out of eggs.

BECAUSE MY AGENT
DIDN'T LIKE IT

Chris Dolley

I sold my first book because my agent didn't like it.

He loved my "A Year in Provence with Miss Marple" book, but when I showed him my SF novel *Resonance*...he wasn't interested. "Could you rewrite it as a medical thriller?" he asked. "Or maybe a political thriller?"

This threw me. Take the SF out of *Resonance* and there's no story. But what do you do if you feel passionately about a book, but your agent hates it?

For me, *Resonance* was *that* book. The special one that writes itself. It came to me in 2000 when three ideas that I'd had kicking around in my head for years suddenly coalesced and I realised they weren't three separate ideas, but three sides of the same story. From there, the book flowed—I outlined it in a matter of hours and the more I fleshed out the book, the more I realised how perfectly the three ideas meshed. For years I'd had a narrator without a story; a mechanism without a plot; and a plot without a purpose. Now I had a book.

But not one my agent wanted to sell.

So...

I parked the book in Baen's electronic slushpile. I didn't want to go through the rounds of finding another agent or dashing off letters to publishers. I just wanted somewhere to put the book so I could feel that I hadn't given up on it, but, at the same time, didn't involve me in extra work. In the meantime, I'd concentrate on my other books.

Two years passed. I parted ways with my agent after we discovered that the expat memoir boom had just burst and all the UK publishers were cutting back on them. I experimented with mystery, writing a quirky detective novel which I entered into Warner's First Mystery Novel contest. It became a finalist.

Then, just as I'd convinced myself that mystery was the way to go, I received an email from Jim Baen.

Many authors have exciting tales about the moment they received "The Call." That email or phone call that contains the magic words—"we want your book."

I didn't so much receive "The Call" as eavesdrop on a conversation about it.

I woke up one morning to find a forwarded email from Jim Baen in my in-tray. It began with a mention of a previous email he'd sent and could I get in touch. Ten other emails (six days of back and forth within Baen) were appended to the bottom, chronicling the attempts to find me, the offer of publication, and fears I may have signed elsewhere.

I had to read it several times. I was 95% sure it was legit—getting up every now and then to execute the Snoopy happy dance and hug the cat—but why the trouble finding me? I'd given them my address, email, and telephone number.

Perhaps it *was* a hoax?

It's worth mentioning here that when I was seventeen I received a hoax letter, purportedly from Penguin, saying that a writing scout had recommended me to them. I believed every word of it. If football clubs could have scouts roaming the playing fields of Britain looking for talent, why couldn't publishers? And recently I'd had my identity stolen and our life savings appropriated, so I was a tad warier than most when it came to unexpected emails.

Then I noticed another email in my in-tray. It was from a

Baen employee telling me that Baen wanted to publish my book, but couldn't find me. I found messages on my website too. A web-wide search was on for the missing author. Where was he? Is he out there?

I was amazed. And wondering if there was time to email Baen an acceptance before I was officially declared dead.

Being in France, I then had to wait a further eight hours for daylight to reach America before Jim Baen could reply. It was worth the wait.

So, that's my story. *Resonance* was the first book to make it out of Baen's electronic slushpile. It was picked up by SFBC and I recently optioned the film rights.

As for my "A Year in Provence with Miss Marple" memoir— the one recounting our first eight months in France, and how, after being abandoned by the police forces of four countries, I had to track down the identity thief myself and bring him to justice—that became *French Fried*, a *New York Times* bestseller.

* * *

Chris Dolley is a *New York Times* bestselling author and a former teenage freedom fighter. That was in 1974 when Chris was tasked with publicizing Plymouth Rag Week. Some people might have arranged an interview with the local newspaper. Chris created the Free Cornish Army, invaded the country next door, and persuaded the UK media that Cornwall had risen up and declared independence. As he told the police at the time, "It was only a small country, and I did give it back."

He now lives in rural France with his wife and a frightening number of animals. They grow their own food and solve their own crimes.

His first Reeves and Worcester Steampunk Mystery— *What Ho, Automaton!*—was a WSFA Small Press Award finalist in 2012.

WITH A LITTLE HELP FROM A POET

Brenda Cooper

Even without seeing the other essays, I believe one theme will be common. We get in our way, we get out of our way, and we get help. What can I say? Before we can write about the hero's journey, we have to live it.

I think I knew I was going to be a writer the day I was born. Coopers do it that way—decide early and follow through. My son told me he was going to be a firefighter when he was five, and what is he now? That's right. My dad wanted to be a rocket scientist. He is. Still. In his eighties. So we Coopers are good, but we're also good at getting in our own way.

~oOo~

I start by getting in my own way

I had a kid (the firefighter) when I was nineteen. The first time I submitted a story I was also nineteen, and at that time about seven months preggers and barefoot and poor in Florida. Poor as in my boyfriend spent the rent money on drugs and we were always a week away from homelessness. This was, by the way, all self-inflicted since I could have been living at home with my nice middle-class family. At any rate, Asimov's rejected the story, saying it was "hackneyed." They even used that word. I had to look it up. It stung. But they also said my writing was good and

I should send them more. I didn't listen—at least not for twenty years. See, at the time I was too stupid to know that was a great rejection. A nineteen-year-old doesn't know what good love is, or good sex, or even a good business idea. How could I have been expected to know what a great rejection was?

So I had my son, and then I had to figure out how to take care of him. No easy feat when you are a kid yourself. I did get to college (with help from my long-suffering but sweet parents). I studied computers, since writing looked unlikely to pay the bills. I wrote poetry then, and published that, but no novels, no stories, nothing but poems.

And journals. I was fourteen the year the "Nothing Book" came out and journaling came in, and I have never stopped. In the next eighteen years I must have filled up fifty journals. Mostly with angsty crap about how I should be writing. WTF? That was writing. I was spending time doing it. I could have used that time to write novels, except I didn't know I could.

Many years later I listened to Ursula Le Guin explain how she wrote with her toddlers beside her on the floor in a playpen, and I cried.

~oOo~

I finally get out of my way

The year my firefighter turned eighteen, I finally realized that I was getting OLD (I wasn't, at least not compared to now, but somehow we humans are always young and stupid). I went back to school. By then I had a bachelor's degree in business, but I wanted to study writing. So I did. The only available creative writing class in Longview Washington in 1997 was at Lower Columbia College, and a poet taught it.

So there I was, a wannabe science fiction writer sitting in a poet's class in a rural town on the industrial edge of the great Columbia River, with a bunch of students who were twenty years younger than me and mostly taking the class since they saw it as an easy three credits.

~oOo~

I get help from my friends

Turns out, Joseph Green loved words. He loved words so much that everyone in the class loved words. You loved words or you dropped out. *And* you were expected to actually write the darned things. So instead of journaling line after line about how miserable it was that I couldn't write, I wrote.

Sounds simple, right?

All those years of writing about writing while not actually writing? Gone. Suddenly writing was *homework.*

I had felt guilty about writing because it was something I wanted to do, but now someone else was telling me it was okay and so I was doing it. Yes, that's sad on many levels. But I wrote my ass off and since I was doing the work I got some credibility.

If I had never taken Joseph Green's class, I would not be a published author today. Classes were Wednesday nights and I started looking forward to them Thursday morning. They were the highlight of my weeks. His love of the written word, of playing with words, and his respect for the power of words touched my journals and my days and my work, and in many ways he is still an influence. When he does a poetry reading up here in Seattle, I try to go.

~oOo~

I get more help from more friends

Backing up, in the middle of those years-lost-to-angsty-journaling I met a man named Steven Barnes. He taught a class called Lifewriting, which goosed me into taking Joe's class. There's a much longer story there, but this is an essay and not a novel. Steve is still teaching people to succeed. Look him up. At any rate, Steve collaborated with Larry Niven. Introductions occurred. Since I now had work, I was posting some of it. I brought Larry my first ever piece of fan mail about a story I wrote in Joe's class, and Larry asked to see the story and immediately saw what was wrong with it. He worked on it, then I worked on it, then he worked on it…and we published it as a collaboration in Asimov's. I've gone on to have my own cover issue of Asimov's and I've published ten books or so and forty or fifty short stories (and only a handful of poems). And all along the way I've had help from my friends. And from a few Asimov's editors.

~oOo~

That's the story of how I learned that writers write, and how a poet helped me get my passion for writing truly on.

* * *

Brenda Cooper writes science fiction and fantasy novels and short stories. Her most recent novel is EDGE OF DARK, from Pyr. Brenda is a technology professional and a futurist, and publishes non-fiction on the environment and the future. Her non-fiction has appeared on Slate and Crosscut and her short fiction has appeared in *Nature Magazine*, among other venues.

See her website at www.brenda-cooper.com.

Brenda lives in the Pacific Northwest in a household with three people, three dogs, far more than three computers, and only one TV in it.

MY FIRST BOOK

Chaz Brenchley

When people ask how many books I've written, I tend to say "It depends how you want to count." This is annoying, I know, but it's also a serious point. Should I include children's books? Short story collections? Novellas? Books written under other names? The abridged children's editions I made of classic novels...?

Similarly, when people ask about my first book, I shrug a little awkwardly and say, "It depends. There are three of them, really." And there really are.

Thing is, I was always very serious about being a writer, and about writing books; and I was never terribly anxious about what sort of books they might prove to be. There were genres I loved—SF and fantasy, largely—but I wasn't proud, and I was willing to write anything. Which is why I was making a living at eighteen, writing teen romances for magazines and comics for kids, while I probed various other avenues to publication. I wanted to write for kids, and for teenagers like myself, and for adults too. I wanted to write novels, of course, but also TV and film scripts and plays and short stories and poetry and and and. It would have helped if I'd actually finished things, but I was young and in a hurry and hence not really getting anywhere.

Then, in my early twenties, I heard that a major London publisher was starting a new line of romantic thrillers, where they provided the storylines and all you had to do was turn a five-thousand-word synopsis into a fifty-thousand-word novel. I could do that, I said. And wrote to the publisher, asking if they were looking for new writers for this exciting project, and if so, here was my track-record. They passed my letter on to the agent whose idea the series was, and who was coordinating everything. She wrote back saying yes, they were definitely looking for new writers, and I sounded interesting, and please write some sample chapters.

So I did that. And she liked them, and the publisher liked them, and they offered me a contract.

I am fond of saying my first novel was commissioned.

They gave me a month, and I panicked because I had never yet actually managed to finish a novel, and wrote the book in three weeks; and I'm still secretly kind of fond of it. But it didn't have my name on, and it wasn't my plot. It was really not my story at all—I didn't even like the story much—and I was obliged to follow their outline to the letter, so I'm really not sure it counts.

And of course I don't want to count it, for all those reasons plus the fact that the series bombed. But the agent said, "Come down and talk to me, it's time you wrote a proper novel anyway." So I went down to talk to her, and we had one of those how-scattershot-am-I conversations. "I read John le Carré, but I don't want to write spy stories; and I read Stephen King, but I don't want to write horror; and I read Dick Francis but I really don't want to write about horses..." When she grew tired of this, she said, "Have you ever read Thomas Harris?" No, I had never heard of Thomas Harris. But she'd just agented *Red Dragon* in the UK, and she thrust a copy into my hands and told me to take it away and read it, because she thought I could do something like it.

Serial-killer thrillers were not yet really a thing, in the UK at least; it was *The Silence of the Lambs* that broke that market open, and that was years away. So I had never read anything like this, and I loved it; and I spent some months thinking about it, and crafting my response to it, and eventually I sent my agent a proposal and some sample chapters. Which she loved, but she thought a commission this time would be unlikely, given that I was starting again from scratch. Go ahead and write the book, she said, and I'll sell it when you're done.

Took me four years, and then a few months more for cuts and rewrites at her insistence; but in the end, she was as good as her word. She sold it to a major house, in a deal for hardcover and paperback both. And that was the first contract I signed for a book that would actually have my name on the cover (actually, initially they were going to go with C R Brenchley, for fear that no one would know how to pronounce Chaz and so never ask for me in bookstores—oh, what a different world it was!—but then the editor forgot to tell the art director, so the cover came with "Chaz Brenchley" all over, and we just ran with it), and surely then this must count as my first book?

Except, um, no. Because see above, under "scattershot": during those four years I was writing a whole lot else as well, including books for kids. And I had a separate agent for the children's work, and she sent a novel I'd actually managed to finish (kids' books are short! and perhaps I had learned something in the meantime) to a publisher, and we didn't hear and didn't hear—until one day I got a fat envelope in the post, and it turned out to contain the typeset proofs and draft illustrations and a cover rough.

So I was quickly on the phone to my agent, "Um, is there something you forgot to tell me?"—and no, not at all, she knew no more about this than I did. It had just entirely slipped the publisher's mind that they perhaps owed us an acceptance letter, and an editorial process, and oh yes, a contract...

They were terribly apologetic. And a contract did follow, but they were so far advanced with the book, that actually came first. And it came out significantly ahead of my beloved serial-killer thriller, so ought really to count as my first proper book. Except that it was an educational publisher who sold direct to schools as part of a literacy programme, so you couldn't actually buy the book in the general trade at all...

So that's the story of my first book, all three of them. Someone else's story under someone else's name; or the kids' book you couldn't buy, that only existed within a proprietary reading-scheme; or the actual novel with my actual name on the cover, available in actual bookshops, that actually came out third. I told you, it just depends how you count.

* * *

Chaz Brenchley has been making a living as a writer since the age of eighteen. He is the author of nine thrillers, two fantasy series, two ghost stories, and two collections, most recently the Lambda Award-winning *Bitter Waters*. As Daniel Fox, he has published a Chinese-based fantasy series; as Ben Macallan, an urban fantasy series. A British Fantasy Award winner, he has also published books for children, two novellas and more than 500 short stories. He has recently married and moved from Newcastle to California, with two squabbling cats and a famous teddy bear. Find him on the internet at www.chazbrenchley.co.uk, and desperance. livejournal.com.

GOING FROM SHORT STORIES TO
NOVELS IN 60,000 EASY WORDS

Tina Connolly

One of the amusing things about my path to publication is that my current agent is also the very first person I ever queried. On a separate project, a year earlier. It was a 12K "chapter book." Please note that at that time I did not yet have my son, who is currently devouring *Magic Treehouse*, *Geronimo Stilton*, and other chapter book series, and I did not really understand the full concept of "chapter book," except that it was a short book for young kids.

At any rate, she rightly sent me a form rejection. A big fat no.

That year was a busy year for me. I had gone to Clarion West a couple years before, and so had leveled up on my short story writing abilities, but I was still stuck on how to write anything longer than a short story. By January of 2007 I had started eighteen novels. (So says my trusty spreadsheet, anyway.) I love worldbuilding and I love characters. I would come up with pages of notes on both of those. And then be utterly stymied at how to make the characters walk across the landscape in anything involving a plot.

I decided to buckle down and apply my Clarion West knowledge. In 2007 I wrote 150K words—twenty-three stories and most of what might sort of be called a novel if you looked at it sideways through a kaleidoscope. It rambled like crazy, and most of the plot pieces didn't connect. That's because my typical method of writing short stories was to write one piece of a jigsaw puzzle and lay it down. Then jump to an entirely different section of the puzzle and stick in another piece that I knew. (Desperately hoping that the two puzzle pieces were from the same puzzle.) At the end: a lot of revision. This works...all right with a 4,000-word short story. It works not at all with an 80K novel.

I needed to attack the novel process in a different way. My longest stories at that point hovered around 6-8K, with a 14K outlier (the story that later became *Ironskin*.) If I was going to figure out how to write longer I needed to start smaller.

Thus the chapter book.

I love kids' books. I love MG and YA. We probably have a thousand kids' books here in the house (most of them mine, from before the kids were born.) So I might not have understood the *current* market back then, but I did love kids' books, and it seemed like a good fit. I wrote the 12K chapter book. Let myself have fun. Finished it in two weeks, right as 2007 closed up shop. (This was super fast for me. I had always thought of myself as a slow writer.)

At any rate, here we were in a new year, and I had completed a full book! It had a plot and everything! I immediately sent out four query letters (including that one to my top agent) and as immediately got four forms.

But that was all right. While I was working on that chapter book, a new idea had sprung into my head, about a wacky girl scientist who was concocting a new kind of chocolate. That poured out, and so did another book, about a class full of horrible kids and a magical lesson. Those stories came in at 20K and 25K—short middle grades perhaps, but still very definitely middle grades. Suddenly it was the end of March and I had three complete manuscripts.

I started querying on those—going about it more thoughtfully this time, making lists of agents and sending queries in batches, refining my title and pitch every time. I was sorry I had burned my "dream" agent by querying her so quickly on that little chapter book—which, by this time, I realized was not correctly aimed at the market. But there were other agents to try.

And also, yay, I had written two 20-25K books, but still, that was not my complete goal. 25K was not a long enough story arc for a YA or adult novel. (Let alone some of the epic trilogies I had made notes about in college—and no, you will never see those.)

And then I got an idea. More correctly, a voice. A quirky, sarcastic girl voice popped into my head. A teenage girl stuck living with a wicked witch, a modern-day Rapunzel.

After my practice with the farcical adventures of the two middle grades, the longer plot of this story practically unrolled itself on the page. I wrote most of the first draft in six weeks. More than anything else, it was *fun*.

Several drafts and a summer of face painting (my excellent and often intense seasonal job) later, it was November, and time to query agents again. I drew up my list, carefully seeding my top choices into little groups so I could tweak the query letter in between. And this time, since it had been eleven months since the first time I had queried her, I decided I could add in my top agent again.

At that time, my agent had a policy that if you didn't hear from her in ten days, then she was passing. (For some reason I had sent her a snail query the first time around. That was back when people did things like that.) At any rate, there we were on day nine and nothing, so I was sure it was another no.

And then I got an email from her. She had fished my query out of her spam filter. She asked for the first fifty pages.

Reader, the rest is history.

Well, except for the part where we failed to sell *Seriously Wicked* the first time around (it was 2009 and no one was buying anything, what can I say,) so then I wrote *Ironskin* and we sold that to Tor in 2010 and it debuted in 2012 and was nominated for a Nebula in 2013 and after I finished out that trilogy with *Copperhead* and *Silverblind* I rewrote *Seriously Wicked* yet again and sold it and two sequels to my same beloved editor, which brings us to now, when *Seriously Wicked*, one of the books of my heart, is out there.[1]

(I say book of my heart because if you take a book and you put in absolutely everything you think is funny, like dragons in RV garages and demons who imitate Elvis and pixies that look like frogs, then you see, you have written a book that only you can write, and I love this book pretty hard for that.)

Of course, the other story I could tell you is about how we sold *Ironskin* and its as-yet-unwritten sequel in November 2010, and then a month later I had my first baby. That's another part of the path to publication, the part that was COMPLETELY SLEEPLESS.

But you can come find me at a con and I'll tell you those stories. At least the ones I remember. There was an awful lot of sleep-deprivation on my path to publication . . . .

* * *

Tina Connolly is the author of the Ironskin trilogy from Tor Books, and the Seriously Wicked series from Tor Teen. Her novels have been finalists for the Nebula and the Norton. Her stories have appeared in *Lightspeed*, *Tor.com*, *Analog*, and more, and are collected in *On the Eyeball Floor and Other Stories*, from Fairwood Press. She is one of the current co-hosts of Escape Pod, and her narrations have appeared all over, including Podcastle, Beneath Ceaseless Skies, and her Parsec-winning flash fiction podcast Toasted Cake. She lives with her family in Portland, Oregon, and her website is tinaconnolly.com.

---

1   *Editor's note: Not only is* Seriously Wicked *out there; it has just been short-listed for a Norton Award.*

MY FINN FANCY ADVENTURE
IN PUBLISHING

Randy Henderson

There are really two stories. The story of how I got published. And the story of why I got published.

Well, there's also the story of how I celebrated getting published, but unless you've already seen the uncensored photos, or joined me in signing the non-disclosure agreement, I can't really speak about it.

So, we'll start with "how":

First, I wrote the opening chapter to a book. Really, I didn't have an entire novel in mind, the chapter was just me having some fun after being burned out on writing an epic (failure) of a YA fantasy novel.

Next, I took my chapter to a writing workshop where it would be critiqued by the amazing Tor editor, Beth Meacham. In the critique, Beth said she'd be willing to read the novel when it was finished—so I decided maybe I should go ahead and actually finish it. And she said she assumed it would follow a mystery plot shape, and I said of course. Then I went home and Googled "mystery plot shape" and started to think about what the rest of the novel might actually be, since all I really had was that crazy opening chapter.

I wrote *Finn Fancy Necromancy* over the next year, and sent it to Beth. I then went to the writing workshop again, this time submitting the opening chapter to what was my next project, since I didn't assume *Finn Fancy* would sell. Agent Cameron McClure was my workshop leader this time, and we hit it off.

A few months after that Beth made me an offer to buy two books. After I stopped dancing around and giggling and crying, I reached out to Cameron and asked if she'd represent me. To her credit, she didn't just say yes to a guaranteed book deal, but insisted on reading the manuscript and thinking about it first before agreeing.

That's the "how," but my experience is not an easily repeatable or guaranteed formula for success. In fact, there is no such thing as a guaranteed formula. Lots of folks go to workshops and have their chapters read by editors or agents without selling them. And lots of folks sell their novels without ever attending a single workshop.

So what is probably more important is the question of "why" I got published.

First, I finished writing a novel. It's amazing how actually finishing a novel makes it easier to sell.

Second, I had a lot of fun writing *Finn Fancy*. It came from my heart, and is full of things I love, things that interest me and that I enjoy. It was not a calculated commercial exercise, or writing in a genre or style that is popular but not my true passion.

Third and finally, the novel I finished was arguably plotted and written decently. For me, this was the end result of years and years of writing stories and novels. I wrote a million words. I wrote hundreds of short stories and two novels before I started to really sell on a professional level. Some people can write their first novel and have it be amazing, but alas that was not me.

Certainly, reading books and attending workshops helped me hone my craft. Clarion West helped me advance years in just six weeks, and introduced me to a group of writers who have been invaluable in the feedback and support they've offered. You can of course grow as a writer and produce amazing stories without a critique and support group, and you can write novels without ever having written a short story, but I personally found that they helped me identify my areas of weakness and opportunities for growth far more quickly than if I'd jumped right into novels and had to figure out on my own why they weren't selling.

Because of course whenever I finished writing a story or novel, I truly believed in it. It is only with time and greater experience that I can see how horrible or, at best, amateurish and unoriginal those stories were.

And while it certainly helps to engage personally with editors and agents, in the end they will still judge your story based on its own merits. They have to live with each book they represent for years, reading it several times, selling and evangelizing it. So they have to truly and personally love a book before they'll take it on. Thus, even if you've had a good conversation with them, and even if you've written a great book, if that novel doesn't resonate with the editor or agent personally then they will pass on it.

In short (too late), the reason "why" I was published was that I did the long, hard work of writing until I became gooder enough at writing that editors began buying my work. I demonstrated a level of professionalism and commitment to being a writer by actually producing finished and edited works, and pursuing opportunities to connect with the community. I was lucky enough to get the right work in the hands of the right editor with whom it resonated. And part of the reason it resonated, I believe, is because it was written from my passions and interests.

So write constantly. Write what you love. Put your work out there. Do this, and success will follow. Eventually.

* * *

Randy Henderson is an author, milkshake conoisseur, Writers of the Future grand prize winner, relapsed sarcasm addict, and Clarion West graduate. His "dark and quirky" contemporary fantasy series which includes *Finn Fancy Necromancy* and *Big-*

footloose and Finn Fancy Free are out now from TOR (US) and Titan (UK). http://www.randy-henderson.com.

JINXED

Elizabeth Bourne

What can you do if your novel is jinxed? This happened to me. This could happen to you. No wait, there is no such thing as a jinx. Well, not usually. Mostly not. But sometimes, it seems there is.

Back in the long ago years, 2008 it was, my historical novel (which for this purpose I'll call *Nights in Carthage*) was finished. The end. I began sending out queries to multiple agents. And finally, I was successful. An agent was interested in my book. Very interested. The agent was the late, great Barbara Bova. She was amazing, and for me, she set the standard for agents. She was professional. She was enthusiastic. She provided amazing feedback. We agreed *Nights in Carthage* should be the first book in a trilogy. We worked together to polish the book. At last, it was done.

At this point, she began contacting editors. Every week, sometimes every few days, she would email me with information on where she'd sent it, who she'd talked to, and what they had said. The third editor who received the package, a senior editor at a major publishing house who shall remain nameless, loved *Nights in Carthage*. She agreed with Barbara that this could be a blockbuster. This, as you can imagine, was wonderful news. I may have fantasy cast my book. I may have visualized seeing my name on the *New York Times* bestseller list. I may have drunk too much champagne. Everything was going great!

Then the senior editor was fired. Terminated. Sent home with her belongings in a box. She was gone, and so was the contract we'd been working on. Her properties were reassigned to other, junior editors. And the junior editor loved my book! She thought it was great! She wanted it. So again, much cheering occurred. Both Barbara and I thought yes! This is it! Everything is go, go, go!

A week later, we received an email from the junior editor. If email could have tear stains, this would have been that email. All acquisitions had been halted. Her division was being merged with another division as their publishing house had been acquired. Or maybe they had done the acquiring. Either way, she could not buy the book. In fact, this was her last email. All her belongings were in a box to take home. She had also been fired.

Barbara did not give up. She'd keep working. It was a great book. It would find a home. I agreed in an absent-minded way as my husband was scheduled for anticipated, major surgery. Which went terribly wrong. So the next email I received from Barbara, I told her that while she was welcome to continue to sending the book out, I did not have the time or emotional energy to deal with *Nights in Carthage*. She was understanding. She sent flowers and chocolates and cards with cute kittens on them.

Six months later, my husband was well enough that I contacted Barbara again. She did not reply. After a few months had passed, I received an email from Ben Bova informing me that his wife had died, and that they were uncertain what to do with her clients. They would let me know. I was shocked and grieved. Barbara was an amazing, wonderful woman, and a great agent. While my loss was not nearly as great as the Bovas', I missed her tremendously.

At last, Ben informed me he had decided to close her agency. The junior agent I had been working with went out on her own, but decided not to represent my book, as her standalone agency was going to concentrate on romances, and my book did not fit.

I decided to hunt for a new agent. In the meantime, I started writing a mystery novel set in San Francisco during Prohibition. After a research trip to San Francisco, my beloved husband died unexpectedly. And that was very nearly the end of everything.

It has taken years to pick up the pieces of my life. In the meantime I have published a number of short stories. I finished two new, completely different novels in 2015. But I have not gone back to *Nights in Carthage*, or the half-written second novel in the trilogy, or the outlined third novel.

So let's go back to that whole jinx business. Are there such things? Maybe, maybe not. But *Nights in Carthage* is a killer. The toll now is two editors, an entire publishing division destroyed, and two deaths. Honestly, I expect the military to approach me any day now with an offer. It might make a great secret weapon.

* * *

Elizabeth Bourne has previously published short fiction in *Fantasy & Science Fiction*, *Clarkesworld*, *Interzone*, and *Black Lantern*. Currently, she is working on a second-world fantasy where luck is real, a mystery set in 1920s San Francisco, and a Viking saga based on Gertrude, Hamlet's mother. Bourne grew up in Lovecraft country and assures you that his work wasn't fiction. She currently lives in Seattle where trolls do, in fact, live under bridges.

MY PATH TO PUBLICATION

John A. Pitts

If you ignore the previous two decades of fits and starts, the degree in English, the decade unlearning "literary snobbery" and the slog of submission/rejection in the short story realm, I had a fairly straightforward path to my first novel sale.

Firstly I met my editor at a convention, Radcon in Tri-Cities, Washington, to be precise. I had a friend, Janna Silverstein, who knew the editor, Claire Eddy from Tor, personally and agreed to give me an introduction. At this point I had one novel written (okay, two, but the novel I wrote when I was fourteen had moved to Florida with my best friend Andy, never to be seen again). I spoke with Claire and Janna for more than an hour in the bar, discussing life things such as children, work, conventions and our favorite things—as one does. I did NOT ask her to read my novel. It felt rude. I was happy to meet her and get to know her a little as a new friend. She is amazing.

After the convention I sent her a short email (as she'd given me her card) and thanked her for the conversation and asked if she was looking for anything particular at the moment.

She replied that I was a nice guy and to send over whatever I had. No requirement for an agent (yet), no firewall of "we only accept solicited manuscripts." Here was a solicitation. I sent her my novel and waited.

Now, it is not unusual to wait one or more years to hear back from a New York editor. They get thousands of manuscripts a year and to slog through them takes a while. Claire got back to me in three months. She rejected the novel, which was a bummer, but she got back to me in three months. That's HUGE. The pros I know were stunned to hear that. Sure, the rejection stung (actually she was very nice and gave me good feedback as to why), but to hear back so quickly from New York was a very rare thing and I should count myself lucky.

A year or so went by and I wrote my second novel, *Black Blade Blues*. WorldCon in Denver was coming up, so I emailed Claire and asked if she or her assistant was going to attend. Alas, she was not, but she said I didn't have to see her face-to-face to send her my next novel. She liked my writing and looked forward to seeing my next book.

That is happy making, let me tell you. I set about polishing that novel to the best of my abilities and sent it off to her just before World Fantasy in Calgary, Alberta, Canada, the fall of 2008.

I attended World Fantasy with a lot of other people and, per my usual introverted self, did my best to intermingle with others but felt like an outsider the whole time. Several times I ran into Claire, but she was always busy. On Saturday, Tor had a room party and me and my friend Michael Hiebert arrived early. They were just setting up so we helped move tables, etc., but the editors appeared harried. It seems that one of their authors had a book turned movie debuting on PBS that very night and they wanted to have the television on to show it. Now, if you weren't aware, I'm six-three and let's just say none of the Tor editors present were even close.

See, the television remote was on top of the credenza and none of them could see it, much less reach it. I stepped up, offering to help and introduced myself just in case. Claire was quick to recognize me and said, "I have your novel on the floor of my office." I said, without thinking, "So you can stand on it to reach high things."

I think she gave me "the look" that most people would recognize from their mom, but she smiled when I handed her the remote. Then the room got crazy and we didn't speak more.

I saw her from time to time, but by the last day, just before the World Fantasy Awards, I had to go pack to leave. I was not going to get my minute to talk to her about my novel and was prepared to just leave. I headed to the elevator to go up to my room when it opened and there stood Claire all alone. She smiled as I got on and struck up a conversation.

I had been in the bar earlier and overheard one of the Penguin editors mention to a friend that she had heard that Tor was looking to purchase some Urban Fantasy. Lo and behold, my novel mostly fit that category. So, as I spoke with Claire, I mentioned overhearing that fact, and she invited me to get off the elevator and stand by the gift shop with her for a few minutes before she went off to the award ceremony. For almost five minutes we discussed my novel and she was intrigued. She said she'd read it and get back to me. I was happy to have given my magical "elevator pitch" and went home thinking the con to be a success.

Six weeks later Claire contacted me about *Black Blade Blues* and from there my first published novel became a reality. The tale from that point forward is interesting. Catch me at a con sometime and I will tell you the next part of the story.

* * *

John A. Pitts is an award-winning author who lives in the Pacific Northwest. In the dead of winter, when not committing novel, he can be found battling the elusive tree squids in the world's only temperate rainforest. During the short summer months, he writes in an attempt to avoid the dreaded glowing ball of fire in the sky.

APRIL IS THE CRUELLEST MONTH

Mindy Klasky

To mangle a Harry Chapin lyric, I got my first agent in the usual way (at least for an author struggling to break into publishing in the early 1990s). I bought a copy of *The Writer's Digest Guide to Literary Agents*, and I pored over the indexes in the back. I determined which agents charged for representation (and immediately crossed them off my list), which agents represented authors of traditional fantasy, and which agents represented authors I had heard of. I steadfastly ignored the little marginal symbol indicating which agents were accepting new clients. I knew that *my* manuscript was so brilliant that every agent would jump at the chance to represent me, even if they were otherwise closed to submissions. In the end, I sent out six query letters, targeting my top prospects.

I quickly received five rejections (one by the then-novel communication method of email!). And within a week, I received a request for a partial from Agent X. That request was followed up by a quick request for a full, and then an offer of representation. I was in heaven.

I'll spare you a long, sad story. Over the next four years, I broke up with Agent X three times. Each time, he told me I'd misunderstood, that we were great together, that we really had something special, and I took him back. All the while, he was shopping around Novel 0 (a traditional fantasy novel, one that is safely trunked beneath my bed, making the world safe for all fantasy readers today).

While I waited for fame and fortune to strike, I started writing a different fantasy novel in a different world with a different cast of characters—featuring a thirteen-year-old female apprentice in a stained-glass-makers' guild who witnesses the assassination of a prince and is accused of being the killer, necessitating her masquerading through her strict caste-bound society to find the true murderer. I finished my draft. I revised my draft. I revised my revision.

And I finally sent it to Agent X.

Who informed me that the new book, now called *The Glasswrights' Apprentice*, "suffered from many of the flaws in [Novel 0]. Alas, there comes a time in every relationship when it's time to move on…"

He broke up with me. After I'd broken up with him three times previously.

He wasn't a total cad, though. He recommended that I approach three other agents. I dutifully sent out my three query letters, only to receive two quick rejections. The third agent, though, responded with an intrigued request for a partial. I sent *Apprentice* to Richard Curtis. He agreed to represent me, and on March 31, 1998, we signed a one-year contract for representation. (Yes. Remember that date. It will be important in a moment.)

Richard was everything I'd missed with Agent X. He was based in New York City. He used computers, including email. He had a large list of currently publishing clients. He kept me informed of submissions, even when that information was a series of rejection letters. He offered advice on possible new projects.

Alas, despite Richard's best efforts, *Apprentice* didn't sell. I accumulated a nice folder full of rejections, nearly a dozen of them. Some were personalized, but most were the vague "doesn't meet our needs at this time" type rejection that is instantly infuriating and ultimately a justification for a pint of Ben and Jerry's.

My contract with Richard expired.

But then, a year and a day after the original contract was signed, I got a phone call from Richard. I was working in my law firm's New York City office, so I wasn't at my desk to take his call. Instead, I received a voice mail message: "Roc at PenguinPutnam is interested in buying *Apprentice*. They want to know if you have a sequel. I told them you have two. Call me."

I didn't have one sequel, of course, much less two. (I *did* have a new fantasy novel, in a completely different world, because I didn't want to be trapped if *Apprentice* never sold.) Hyperventilating, I phoned Richard, only to discover that he'd gone home for the day. I left a message, asking him to call me in the morning.

I'd done everything I could do. Because I was in New York, and because I wasn't about to sit alone in my hotel room holding my good news close to my chest, I headed out to see a Broadway play. I bought half-price tickets for *Night Must Fall*, and as the curtain rose, I watched a naked Matthew Broderick stumble around on stage in the midst of stage-effect thunder and lightning.

And there, in the darkness of the theater, I was struck by my own bolt out of the proverbial blue.

It was April 1. April Fool's Day.

What if Richard's phone message was a terrible joke, one that he told to all of his authors after their contracts expired? A book and two sequels? That had sounded too good to be true. Now, I understood why.

I barely resisted the urge to leave the theater then and there. (Honestly, I should have. The play wasn't very good.) I wandered back to my hotel after the show, asking myself over and over and over again—is the offer real? I barely slept that night, alternating between imagining plots for two sequels and imagining the end of my writing career before it had ever truly begun.

In the bleak light of dawn on April 2, I headed back into the office, nursing coffee from a street cart and a bagel with a shmear.

I counted down the seconds until I could call Richard's office. I pressed the ten digits on the precise stroke of eight a.m.

Richard answered the phone himself. Without any preamble, I asked, "Are you the cruellest man in the world?"

When he was through laughing, he assured me that the offer was real. We talked about strategies for negotiating the contract. Ultimately, I signed on the proverbial bottom line—a three-book contract for *The Glasswrights' Apprentice*, a sequel, and a third book to be named later (the unrelated fantasy novel I'd written while waiting to hear about *Apprentice*).

The Glasswrights' Apprentice was released in July 2000. One month later, Roc offered me a new contract for three more Glasswrights books. I've gone on to publish more than two dozen novels.

But I still have an unexpected love for April Fool's Day, even though (*especially* though) I despise the playing of pranks!

* * *

USA Today bestselling author Mindy Klasky learned to read when her parents shoved a book in her hands and told her she could travel anywhere through stories. As a writer, Mindy has traveled through various genres, including hot contemporary romance. In her spare time, Mindy knits, quilts, and tries to tame her to-be-read shelf. Visit her at www.mindyklasky.com.

I WAS REJECTED, THEN SOLD THE SAME STORY TO THE SAME EDITOR!

Amy Sterling Casil

My path to publication would have been very different, and may never have happened, if I hadn't entered the L. Ron Hubbard Writers of the Future contest between 1995 and 1998. Eventually, I ended up winning two prizes and attending the Writers of the Future events in Hollywood in 1998 and 1999. But my first professional publication wasn't a story entered in the contest; it came as a result of it, especially help from the head judge: Dave Wolverton (who also writes fantasy novels as David Farland). Another judge of this contest, Kathy Wentworth, was a writer and editor beloved by many. Kathy suffered from cancer and died in 2012. At that time, Dave Wolverton returned as the head judge. He is currently the judge of this contest, which continues to help new and aspiring writers and artists.

Back in those long-ago days, we still sent work in the mail, whether on submission to a print publisher, or to a contest like Writers of the Future. The idea of "simultaneous submissions" was very important. Most publications didn't want them. What if you sent a physical story to six different publications, and more than one of them agreed to publish the work? You ran the risk of "being banned" if editors learned you were trying to save time and postage by taking a "simultaneous submission" shortcut.

The preferred method was to laboriously put the printed story in a manila envelope and include a self-addressed, stamped envelope for the response—you could either include a large manila envelope in which the editor could return the actual manuscript, or a small, regular white envelope, which would be big enough for a form letter response. The understanding with the small envelope was that the editor could throw away or recycle the manuscript you had sent and just return a note or form letter.

Think about the cost in time, effort, postage and paper!

So, why was I doing this? Starting in junior high, I had the crazy idea I wanted to be a science fiction writer. By the time I was in college, I read an article in *Asimov's* magazine urging young writers to apply to the Clarion Science Fiction Writers Workshop—at the time held at Michigan State University. I completed a storylike document by mixing and matching what I understood (not very much!) of a literary story by the well-known author Paul Bowles with the plot of one of my favorite Star Trek episodes. I sent this thing to the workshop and they let me in!

Many of the others at the Clarion Workshop were writing fantasy or horror, so I decided, "I want to be a horror writer!" Stephen King was very popular at the time—it seemed like the thing to do. This outstanding thought process resulted in my "pudding I left in the refrigerator came alive and ate everyone!" phase. One of my Clarion classmates convinced me to send my stories to the high-paying, and, to me, very intimidating, *Twilight Zone* magazine. I sent three stories to them. I also sent several others to less-intimidating, low-paying publications and all were rejected. Considering these tales were mostly about deadly pudding, I can't blame these editors. I got used to seeing a big manila envelope in the mailbox that I had addressed to myself. Rejection, rejection, rejection.

Because I knew no other writers to talk to after Clarion, I didn't know that I was "getting close" and receiving personal rejections even for malevolent pudding tales—so when I got a rejection card from *Twilight Zone* editor Alan Rodgers*, I decided, "You don't have what it takes, Amy—just forget about it. Devote your time to a real paying job and your family."

I quit writing for eight years.

After my daughter Meredith was born, her father Mike encouraged me to start writing again since it seemed like my life was consumed 100% by our daughter, my ailing father and grandmother, and job/household duties. I needed something to take my mind off of these heavy responsibilities. Mike reminded me, "Didn't you want to be a science fiction writer?"

"Yes," I told him—that was true. I had and did.

Mike pulled out some of his old paperbacks, including *Tales of Known Space* by Larry Niven. As I read, I realized I remembered reading most, if not all, of these stories from the old days. I discovered the ability to complete an actual story text—and I didn't have to combine a literary writer's tale with Star Trek, either. I plugged along, writing from 5:00 to 7:00 a.m. before it was time to take Meredith to school.

Rejection. Rejection. Rejection. Forty-two of them. But they were "personal"—i.e., written notes from various editors. I knew enough by this time to know that this meant my work wasn't completely abominable.

I also learned about the Writers of the Future Contest, and the prizes looked great. A lot of writers I respected and admired were either judges, or had won the contest. So I developed a policy: I'd send a story to all the high-paying professional sci-fi markets in order of which ones I thought had the best potential of buying it. If, by the end of this laborious procedure, the story still hadn't sold—then I'd enter it in the contest.

The first story that fit in this category was "Jonny Punkinhead." This story is also my first professional science fiction and fantasy sale. It appeared in the "New Writers Issue" of *The Magazine of Fantasy & Science Fiction* in June, 1996.

When I finished "Jonny Punkinhead" in early 1995, I knew

that I'd "done something." From what I could determine at that time, it was "publishable." Inside, I knew that I'd done the very best that I could do. Through this story, I began to learn what I was really good at as a writer. It was about a subject very close to my heart: inspired by the homeless, desperately poor children I worked with through my day job at that time—the director of a charity devoted to helping people in need. I invented the idea of "changed children," and did much research on slow viruses and genetic mutations to come up with a scenario by which such a disaster might occur. I left all of this background information out of the story and instead wrote about what might happen if somebody...oh, somebody like me...had to try to take care of these kids who were throwaways—the unwanted, the unloved, the bizarre. Kids with heads like pumpkins and three eyes. Kids like Jonny Punkinhead.

For reasons that are clear to me today (but were unclear to me at the time), I made the protagonist a male doctor—Dr. Hedrick Arlan. At the time, I didn't really understand what I was doing, although I knew the doctor's problems with "taking his job home" were similar to challenges I also faced in my real-world job.

I put "Jonny Punkinhead" in a big manila envelope, along with a self-addressed, folded large manila envelope for its return, and sent it out (one at a time) to every reputable science fiction and fantasy magazine that existed at that time. Guess what happened?

Yeah—same as the Malevolent Pudding stories. Two of the editors, who shall forever remain nameless, actually used these words: "This is an award quality story, but..."

But—they still rejected it.

"Jonny" was rejected by Kristine Kathryn Rusch, at that time the editor of *The Magazine of Fantasy & Science Fiction*.

After all these rejections, I entered it in the Writers of the Future contest. One day, I went to the mailbox and here was another big manila envelope. I trudged back inside and put the envelope on the kitchen counter. I figured, "Another rejection." The same thoughts I'd had eight years before flooded my mind. "Just quit. You're no good. You'll never sell a story."

I cleaned the kitchen before opening the envelope, quickly recognizing "Jonny Punkinhead."

Then a letter fell out. It was pretty long—several pages and typed, single-spaced!

The letter was from Dave Wolverton, head contest judge. "Fred Pohl and I both thought that this was the first prize winner," he wrote. Dave went on to discuss my story in detail, my writing in detail, and by the time I finished, I could hardly breathe. Even then, though, I was still thinking, "You didn't win anything and they're sending the story back, unpublished."

Dave said that the story was "publishable." That was great! He urged me to send it to *The Magazine of Fantasy & Science Fiction,* where he felt it would be a "good fit."

He had no way to know that the story had already been sent to that magazine and rejected.

Keep in mind this was before regular use of the internet and I didn't know what to do. How could I send a story back that had already been rejected even if Dave Wolverton said it was good and right for the publication? Then I read Fred Pohl's letter. You may not know who Fred Pohl is, but if you love science fiction, he was the author of *The Space Merchants*, *Man Plus*, and the Gateway novels. He was also the editor of *Galaxy* magazine, and considered to be the best editor in the field for many years. As I read this letter, I knew that Fred Pohl had picked a number of incredibly successful, wonderful writers of short science fiction out of his editorial slush pile. Among them, he had "discovered" Cordwainer Smith—and as far as I was concerned, Cordwainer Smith was a genius.

Fred Pohl's letter was much shorter than Dave Wolverton's, but he said, "Being able to read stories like this is why I have continued to judge this contest over the years." He called my story "award-quality" and my writing "beautiful," and I believed him. That was when I decided not to quit.

As far as my "but the story was already rejected" dilemma, I wrote Dave Wolverton back. Following his guidance, I put the story back in an envelope, wrote a new cover letter that said, "Dave Wolverton suggested I send this to you," and sent "Jonny Punkinhead" back to Kristine Rusch at *The Magazine of Fantasy & Science Fiction*. Honestly, I didn't change a word, though the cover letter probably said "I revised this with Dave's advice" (in fact, I'm certain I said that—he told me to!).

And this time, she bought it.

I kept writing. It took me a long time—two years, probably—to recapture the feeling I had when I wrote "Jonny Punkinhead." I wrote competent, even moving stories in the meantime. But stories like "Jonny" don't come every day. Stories like that come from heartfelt honesty, caring, and sincerity. How many words had I written before I wrote "Jonny"? I'm not sure. It wasn't the "million words" that I heard bestselling author Harry Turtledove speak of—he said that writers had to write a million words before they became publishable, professional writers. I racked up a total of eighty rejections before my next professional sale.

No one can take "Jonny Punkinhead" from me, or tell me that he's not a winner, because I know that little boy is a winner, even if he lost hope in his own story. Even if he smashed his own head against the wall just the way I wanted to do back then.

~oOo~

My grandfather always told me, "You have to take the bad with the good." When I was growing up and reading science fiction, my ultimate dream was to be a part of *The Magazine of Fantasy and Science Fiction*, which was the place where all the writers I most loved and admired published their work. Ray Bradbury, Harlan Ellison, Daniel Keyes, Walter M. Miller. Writers like that. My writing has been sandwiched in issues between writers like

Ursula K. Le Guin and Joyce Carol Oates. That's not "the bad." That's "the good."

And that *asterisk? *Alan Rodgers, the *Twilight Zone* editor? I met him in 1998, not realizing who he was until quite a while after he and I had fallen in love. We were either a couple, or very close friends, until his untimely death after a series of strokes in 2014. I had kept the little card he'd sent as a rejection—the one that convinced me to quit writing way back when.

When I showed it to him and told him the story of how the terse, small card had inspired me to quit, he said, "Amy, I only wrote six or seven of those the whole time I was at *Twilight Zone*. That was meant to encourage you. If you had sent another story as good as that one, I probably would have bought it!"

* * *

Amy Sterling Casil is a 2002 Nebula Award nominee and recipient of other awards and recognition for her short science fiction and fantasy, which has appeared in publications ranging from *The Magazine of Fantasy & Science Fiction* to *Zoetrope*. She is the author of 28 nonfiction books, over a hundred short stories, three fiction and poetry collections, and three novels. Amy is a founding member and treasurer of Book View Café author cooperative, and former treasurer of the Science Fiction & Fantasy Writers of America. She teaches at Saddleback College and is a founder of a new publishing company for the 21st century, Chameleon Publishing.

THE MAGIC PHONE CALL

Deborah J. Ross

It's the moment every struggling-to-break-in writer dreams about. You've sweated through revision after revision; you've endured and celebrated the feedback from your critique group or trusted reader. You've haunted your own Inbox, dreading and hoping at the same time. To your query, the editor or agent replies, "Yes, we received it. Yes, it's still under consideration."

Still? Calloo callay! Agony of agonies...

The waiting comes to an end, as all things must. This time, it's not with a form rejection or even the more personalized, encouraging "almost there" notes you've been getting. It's a *phone call*! Is there ever a time when you most want to be cool and collected, to savor each microsecond, and yet find your brain inhabited by swarms of frantic, deafening flying things? To quote one of my daughters' favorite books: "What do you say, dear?"

Times have changed since I found myself on the receiving end of such a glorious call. Way back when, such conversations used telephone or postal mail, not email. Conventional wisdom has swung away from "first sell, then get an agent." However, I believe the advice I was given and the ways in which I responded still apply.

First of all, I was of the "sell first, then agent" school. I did not and still do not believe that it is impossible to sell a first novel without an agent. You don't have to agree with me; after all, I could be wrong. I also believed that I could get a much better agent—in fact, the agent of my dreams—if I began with a novel for which an offer had already been made. It didn't bother me in the least that an agent would pocket his or her commission without selling the book. I am right up there with the world's ten lousiest negotiators. I also wanted an agent who would take the long view, not a single novel sale but my future career.

By the time that magic phone call came, I had done considerable homework. I'd regularly read essays by various agents. I'd met writers I admired and, after sufficient trust was established, asked them about their experiences with agents. I wasn't looking for horror stories, but a sense of each agent's philosophy, the way he or she interacted with authors. I considered how similar my work was to that of the other writer. I composed my dream list. And waited. And submitted. And waited some more. And wrote several more novels while waiting.

At last came a call from my editor. "I've finished reading your book," she said. "I love your work."

Pause.

I squeaked, "Does this mean…" *I'm going to sound sooo stupid if I'm wrong!* "…you want to buy it?"

She laughed.

The world turned inside out. With very little oxygen reaching my brain, I stammered, "This is so wonderful, I can hardly breathe. I'm so glad you like it! I can't think about numbers… you'll have to discuss that with my agent."

"Great. Have him call me."

In stupefaction, I hung up the phone. What had I done? I didn't have an agent!

I picked up the phone and dialed the office of the agent at the top of my list. He was in. He was happy to take my call. "I've just gotten an offer for my first novel," I said. "I've heard wonderful things about you from Author A, Author B, and Author C. Could you…er, um…negotiate the contract for me?"

"Only if we establish agent-author representation. For all your work."

"Oh. Yes, please."

Then he laughed. Although I was delirious with joy, I was also feeling a bit idiotic. *Why was everyone laughing at me?* It turned out that those same authors had been telling *him* about *me*, and he'd been waiting for me to ask him.

Lessons: Do your homework. Learn the field. Keep writing while you wait. Respect your strengths and weaknesses. Be friendly. And never, *ever* negotiate with your brain on endorphins.

By the way, I'm still with my wonderful agent. The book was *Jaydium*, which you can find on Book View Café and other ebook retailers.

* * *

Deborah J. Ross writes and edits fantasy and science fiction. Her most recent books include *The Children of Kings* (with Marion Zimmer Bradley); Lambda Literary Award Finalist/Tiptree Award recommended list *Collaborators* (as Deborah Wheeler); and *The Seven-Petaled Shield,* an epic fantasy trilogy. Her short fiction has appeared in *F & SF, Asimov's, Star Wars: Tales From Jabba's Palace, Realms of Fantasy,* and *Sword & Sorceress.* Her work has earned Honorable Mention in *Year's Best SF,* and nominations for Gaylactic Spectrum Award, the National Fantasy Federation Speculative Fiction Award for Best Author, the Nebula Award, and inclusion in the Locus Recommended Reading and *Kirkus* notable new release lists. She served as Secretary to the Science Fiction Fantasy Writers of America (SFWA) and is currently on the Board of Directors of Book View Café. When she's not writing, she knits for charity, plays classical piano, studies yoga, and rehabilitates service dogs.

blog: http://www.deborahjross.blogspot.com/
website: http://www.sff.net/people/deborahjross/
BVC Author Page: http://bookviewcafe.com/bookstore/bvc-author/deborah-j-ross/

MY ROAD TO PUBLISHING
OR
TIPTOEING THROUGH
MINE FIELDS

Phyllis Irene Radford

A long time ago, in a galaxy far, far away, I began my publishing career in the most traditional of paths. Way back when, publishing options were much more limited than today. We could submit to a big publisher in New York or Toronto. Or we could pay money for a small vanity press to produce a few hundred copies that would sit in the garage until we hand sold them to an audience that sneered at a writer "not good enough" for traditional publishers. The internet had barely been invented and e-books were still a distant dream.

When I first started taking my writing seriously, a friend of a friend of a friend referred me to Romance Writers of America. The local chapter had monthly meetings with guest speakers and a mid-month workshop on some aspect of writing, like plotting or character development, or for advanced writers, point of view, voice, and pacing. I went to the first plotting workshop and returned home to completely rewrite the book I thought was ready to submit.

They introduced me to my first critique group and taught me to write as well as the business of writing.

Two years into this game, the national RWA conference was

held in San Francisco. A member of my critique group, and a dear friend to this day, organized the agent and editor interviews for the conference. I couldn't afford to attend but a new agent (out of business now and moving on to another career) hungry for clients gave a stack of her business cards to my friend with a request to pass them on to anyone she thought could benefit from her services.

I got one of those cards.

My query letter came back with a positive response. Yes she would like to see my work. I sent her a complete romance novel—aimed at the Harlequin American imprint—and the first half of a very rough draft of a fantasy novel. The fantasy was my therapy book, never intended to sell. A week later the agent called and told me she'd market the romance, but I must finish and polish the fantasy ASAP. That book was where my voice and talent belonged.

It took me another year to finish and polish the fantasy. Meanwhile the romance picked up rejection after rejection: Too much plot, not enough romance; too many ghosts, not enough romance; too much of that crazy woo-woo stuff, not enough romance.

Then *The Glass Dragon* went out to editors all over New York. Twenty rejections later, Sheila Gilbert at DAW Books had read the first three chapters and liked what she read. But… she could see it was not ready for publication. It needed revisions. She and the agent agreed that Sheila should call me. We talked for an hour and agreed that I should revise the first 100 pages, mostly to see if I was capable of doing revisions to her specifications. I did and returned it to her. In the meantime I revised the rest of the book along those same lines.

Six months passed and Sheila had not read my revisions. So the agent sent the completely revised book to more editors and told Sheila what she had done. Within three weeks I had three offers for *The Dragon Nimbus Series*. The best offer came from DAW Books. My agent more than earned her commission on that sale on the difference between the first offer and what we accepted.

Twenty-one years and thirty-eight books later (including three collections of my short stories) publishing has changed. I still write for DAW, but I also write independently and for small press. My books come out as e-books as well as print. And I still haven't run out of ideas or the will power to finish what I write and submit it.

Does my previous success help me continue my career? To a degree. It opens a few doors, but doesn't guarantee acceptance. I still have to work hard to make sure each project is the best I can make it. I still have to research markets—with the help of my new agent—and introduce myself politely to editors I meet at conventions. Writing is a business, after all. And it doesn't wait for me to play catch up.

Writing is also a business where I don't have to retire until I run out of ideas. That should be about two years after I'm in my grave.

* * *

Irene Radford has been writing stories ever since she figured out what a pencil was for. A member of an endangered species—a native Oregonian who lives in Oregon—she and her husband make their home in Welches, Oregon, where deer, bears, coyotes, hawks, owls, and woodpeckers feed regularly on their back deck.

A museum-trained historian, Irene has spent many hours prowling pioneer cemeteries deepening her connections to the past. Raised in a military family, she grew up all over the US and learned early on that books are friends that don't get left behind with a move. Her interests and reading range from ancient history, to spiritual meditations, to space stations, and a whole lot in between.

Mostly Irene writes fantasy and historical fantasy including the bestselling Dragon Nimbus Series. In other lifetimes she writes urban fantasy as P.R. Frost or Phyllis Ames, and space opera as C.F. Bentley. Later this year she ventures into Steampunk as someone else. Find her at www.ireneradford.com.

HOW I BECAME A "REAL AUTHOR"

Sara Stamey

I was always a storyteller, driving my family crazy on car trips by recounting every detail of my colorful dreams. My Grandma Sara helped focus my ambition by playing the card game "Authors" with me, and I decided I would be a Real Author, too, when I grew up. I started by writing illustrated stories of kids who stowed away in a rocket to the moon and rode giant caterpillars while licking pills that turned into ice cream cones.

Graduating high school, I listened to the advice of everyone telling me what "I should do," and studied science instead of writing. Uninspired, I dropped out and became a certified nuclear reactor operator, among other jobs, but finally decided I needed to pursue my dream. Returning to university, I wrote my first novel while finishing my degree in English and Creative Writing. It was science fiction about a far-future "prodigal daughter," titled *Homeworld Stranger*.

Again forgetting the advice of what "I should do" to get published, I sent the novel to a couple of publishers, but gave up after two or three rejections. The note from Ace/Berkley said the story had "too much emotion for science fiction," probably because it had a female protagonist who didn't act like a man or a helpless bimbo. (This was in the mid-1980s, mind you.) I tossed the manuscript into a box and went on some extended travels. When I finally returned to my home town to excavate my storage boxes, my then-partner said, "That's a good novel. Send it out again." Having forgotten where I'd already submitted it, I sent it again to Ace/Berkley. Major publishers at that time were still accepting unagented manuscripts, and if I'd had an agent, she almost certainly would not have duplicated the submission.

Anyway, I got a phone call from new editor Beth Fleisher: "We'd like to publish your novel." Dancing around while trying to hold the phone and sound professional, I accepted the modest advance, then broke out the champagne. I had arrived!

When the contract arrived, I didn't understand much of the legalese, but signed without questioning anything. Luckily ebooks didn't exist yet, so I didn't end up signing away crucial rights and was later able to get all my rights reverted to me. Beth had mentioned that I might have to make "a few revisions," and I then realized that the contract called for cutting 20% of the word count. Back then, most editors still actively edited, and it was a productive learning experience working with Beth to tighten the storyline. A couple of my "darlings" needed to be killed, but I had to admit the novel did benefit.

Berkley changed the title from *Homeworld Stranger* to the jazzier *Wild Card Run*. (My prodigal daughter character is a gambling-game designer who becomes a "wild card" in a high-stakes conflict between humans and controlling "cyber" entities.) They encouraged me to expand it into a series, which I did, and received encouraging reviews from *Publishers Weekly, Locus,* and others. I'm even listed in some science fiction databases as an early Cyberpunk author, along with William Gibson and Neal Stephenson, which tickles me. Unfortunately, when my third novel *Double Blind* was ready for release, Putnam/Berkley/Ace/ etc. was going through another merger, and they somehow forgot to place the books into their distribution system. The entire print run sat in a warehouse somewhere, while various bookstore staff were calling me to ask why they couldn't get orders placed. I had acquired an agent by that time, but she failed to address the issue, and I was booked on a flight to the remote Honduran island where I lived seasonally as a scuba guide, so my career sort of floated away on the tide.

(For those not in the know, book sales are tracked in the industry by computerized systems, and the plunge in my sales numbers meant no one was willing to take me on when Berkley/Ace declined to continue with me after their "mishap" with distribution.)

Such is the life of an author. But these days we have many alternatives to the "Big Five" New York publishers, and I'm happy to have found a home at Book View Café cooperative publishing group, where I'm releasing new novels, as well as reissues of my original "Wild Card" series. I'm working alongside wonderfully talented writers who are helpful and mutually supportive, and finding new readers. Full circle in my dream of being a Real Author—life is good!

* * *

Sara Stamey—award-winning novelist, independent editor, and senior instructor of creative writing at Western Washington University—has returned to her Pacific Northwest roots after years of wanderlust. Her journeys include treasure hunting and teaching scuba in the Caribbean and Honduran islands; backpacking in Greece, South America, New Zealand, and the Northwest; operating a nuclear reactor at Hanford; and owning a farm in Southern Chile. Now resettled in Bellingham, WA, she shares her Squalicum Creek back yard with wild creatures and her cats, dog, and very tall husband Thor.

Her new novel THE ARIADNE CONNECTION won the Cygnus Speculative Fiction Award, and her ISLANDS won the Chanticleer Paranormal Suspense Award. "A stomping, vivid ride." (*Statesman Journal*)

Find her novels at www.bookviewcafe.com and visit her website/blog at www.sarastamey.com.

MAKING IT

Trisha Leigh/Lyla Payne

I decided I wanted to "make it" as a published author back in the days of paper query letters and SASE's—the stone age, really, although Twitter popped on the scene within a year and made everything more accessible and less of a mystery. Still, the path to publication was singular and narrow. If a person wanted to publish a book, there were a set of steps to follow, and one was not to pass go or collect any paltry royalties without first enlisting the belief of a literary agent.

This task is not for the faint of heart. It involves first writing a book that you believe is good enough to be published. After that, research into which agents might be a good fit, crafting a letter that boils your amazing book into three paragraphs, and what seems like an endless number of email refreshes (and whiskey), what do you get?

If you're like me, a towering pile of rejections! Whee!

We will not speak of the first novel I queried. We *may* speak of the first novel I queried that *deserved* to be queried, the one that got me not one or two, but three calls from agents who wanted to represent my work.

I talked to them all, picked one, and notified all of my writer friends on Twitter—I had officially made it! Nothing could stop me now, because I had an agent and that meant a giant book deal and movie rights and, possibly, a relationship with Zac Efron, if

I played my cards right. The sky was the limit, now that I'd made it to the big time, right?

Wrong.

Turns out I made a terrible decision when I picked my agent. Not only would she have my revisions for literally months at a time without a response, but we "worked together" for almost a year and my book never went on submission. Meanwhile, YA dystopian blew up and then tanked (yeah, that fast, at least as far as editors were concerned).

It got to the point where I had to do the unthinkable—fire my agent. *Un*-make it, and by my own hand, to boot.

Firing her was the right decision. After I left, she ended up quitting the business and not bothering to tell anyone, not even her bigger clients. The authors who had books on submission never knew what editors they had been to, or even if she'd been honest about submitting the books at all. She stopped answering emails, and there was no chance that someone else at the firm would take any of us on. We were orphaned, and even though I felt the slightest big smug (I'm not perfect, okay?) about leaving before the end, it didn't change the fact that we were all again in the same agentless boat.

I'd made friends on Twitter and in other places with authors and agents, even a few editors, and it seemed like everyone was moving forward. They'd gotten agents, they'd sold manuscripts, they had cover reveals and ARCs and release days and tours, but not me. I queried the book again, but because of the shift in the market, no agents thought they had a chance in hell of selling anything that looked remotely dystopian.

Those were dark times in my life. I can smile and joke about it now, but I thought about quitting. I was depressed, sure that I'd missed my one single chance and the universe had realized somehow that I'd never deserved it to begin with.

About a year before the bottom fell out, when I was signing with an agent, one of my good friends and critique partners had made a bold decision that I had been sure was the wrong one—she'd decided to self-publish a novel.

Now, this is still the relative dark ages, remember? So, self-publishing was a stepchild no one wanted to acknowledge. The only people who did it were people not good enough to make it the right way. They couldn't get agents, they couldn't sell books, so they gave up—at least, that's what established authors and agents and editors wanted us to believe. Hell, maybe they wanted to believe it, too.

And that wasn't me. It wasn't what I dreamed of and it wasn't what I had been told over and over that making it as a published author looked like.

But now, a year later, that well-worn path hadn't worked for me. I *knew* my book was good—it had gotten interest from three agents when I'd queried the first time. The second time it made the query rounds, none of my responses were negative. Everyone liked the book, but dystopian was over and they didn't think they could sell it.

Long story short (I know, too late!), it broke my heart to think of shelving the book…so I didn't. I took the knowledge my friend had amassed over the previous twelve months and decided to self-publish the book.

Was I excited about it? No. I cried, I felt like a failure, and figured it probably meant the end of my chances to ever be a successful author in the eyes of the publishing community.

Here's what I didn't know: the publishing community was already undergoing a change, whether it wanted to or not. The shift began with the emergence of ebooks, and continued with their rise in popularity, especially in certain genres. Not only was it changing, the publishing community was expanding to include other people, like my friend and me, who were self-publishing products that could compete with books that had gone through the traditional process in every single way.

To accomplish that, we invested in the books up front. I paid multiple types of editors, hired cover designers who also had done books for the "Big Five," used professional formatters and made sure there were print versions available. Some of the best compliments I received, early on, were from readers who said "I would never have guessed this was self-published."

The book started to sell, and I completed the series. The New Adult category exploded and I decided to throw my hat in the ring, starting a second series that would not only allow me the financial freedom to quit my job, but let me put the nifty little "USA Today Bestselling Author" in front of my name. Being a successful self-published author started to feel good, not shameful. I was proud of the books I had available. I was making more money and putting out more titles than my friends who had decided to go the traditional route (but I was investing more, too, monetarily); but best of all, I was learning *so much* about publishing as a business.

It's been over four years since I took those depressed, hesitant steps into self-publishing, where I've found an unexpected home in a community of hardworking business people. I've learned, mostly through trial and error, about creating books, marketing books, selling books, and branding myself as an author. I've had amazing months and terrible months, as far as sales, and I've tried to learn from them both. I've signed three traditional book deals (and cried with disappointment over one the same way I did the decision to self-publish), because I believe the author of the future will be successful only by having multiple avenues to get their work into the hands of readers.

And guess what? I don't feel like I've made it anywhere but to a place where I'm confident in my ability to continue writing. There is no *making it*—no magical land where there's nowhere else to go because the sky is pressing on my head, my hands are full of money, and all the readers I want are waiting for the next book.

That's the secret no one tells you about the path to publishing a book. There is nowhere to arrive, no true destination where dreams end.

No one ever feels as though they have made it.

Not JK Rowling, not Stephen King, not Stephenie Meyer… not if they want to keep growing and keep creating, keep reaching farther for different and better goals.

It's scary, to live a creative life, because it means accepting that as long as we're growing, the finish line is always moving. When I started, my goal was to become a published author via the traditional route. My road has zigzagged through valleys and peaks and more valleys, but it got me to that goal—and past it to new ones—all the same. I have faith that it will continue to take me further, and to greater heights, in the same way.

* * *

Trisha Leigh is from the Midwest, and figures she would have started writing books sooner had anyone thought to tell her it could be an actual job, and not only something fun to do in her spare time. She is the author of three young adult science fiction series (so far), *The Last Year*, *The Cavy Files*, and *The Historians*. She also authors adult books under the name Lyla Payne. Some are romance (*Whitman University*), most are mysteries (*Lowcountry Mysteries*), and a few are thrillers (*Secrets Don't Make Friends*). If you like holiday romance, she's got those, too! Check out *Mistletoe & Mr. Right*! When she's not writing (ha!) Trisha loves hanging with her dogs, baking bread, and enjoys traveling and staying home with family in equal measure. You can find out more at both trishaleigh.com and lylapayne.com, or on any social media platform you prefer—just look for trishaleighkc!

AFTERWORD

THE "USUAL" WRITER'S RÉSUMÉ
OR
YOUR EDITOR'S TALE (TO DATE)

Shannon Page

Years 0-Teenage: I wrote stories in crayon on construction paper when my peers were drawing pictures. I voraciously consumed story—library books, school books, anything I could get my hands on. Journal-keeping began at age eleven, with a lengthy description of a rather wacky Fourth of July (all of which was true).

High School Years: It wasn't called fan fiction then, but that's what I was doing: writing the further adventures of characters I loved in worlds I didn't want to leave just because the silly author had decided that the book should end. My own original work consisted of short stories with shocking twist endings like "and then I woke up." I started novels, abandoning them after ten pages; wrote anguished journal entries; composed execrable poetry. My greatest work of classroom fiction was a book report on an invented book. I had been too busy reading books that didn't fit the narrow parameters of the assignment, so I made one up—publisher and all. I got an A.

College Years: Many, many essays for my Rhetoric major, culminating in an honors thesis outlining in great detail how all the members of the Bloomsbury Group slept with each other (including a hand-drawn diagram).

Early Adulthood: I got busy doing life, I mean collecting material for my writing; still journaling, of course.

Early Thirties: I started to take writing a little more seriously, joining a gentle group of 'women who write'. I wrote a few very bad short stories, and began more aborted novels.

Mid-Thirties: My first completed novel, *Eel River Park and Lodge*, was printed on clean paper, sent to Farrar, Straus and Giroux, and received a polite rejection. With a shrug, I produced a xeroxed spiral-bound copy of the book for friends and family, some of whom read it.

Later Thirties: I started more projects (one of which, *Nightcraft*, I am still working on to this day). I added a monster to *Eel River Park and Lodge* and completely redrafted the novel, now just named *Eel River,* during thirty days in November 2006 for the National Novel Writing Month. I joined two formal critique groups, and finally met other dedicated writers. I began working harder on short stories, having discovered (via this newfangled thing called the Internet) that having a strong short story publication record was the True and Accepted Path to Fame and Fortune.

Early Forties: I did NaNoWriMo a few more times, producing an impressive string of unfinished, unpublished, badly broken novels, including a few more *Nightcraft* variations. I even sold a short story! It was called "Big Muddy," but after several years the anthology had still not come together, and the publisher had still not paid or even sent a contract, so I withdrew it. (A fail-sale. It's still unpublished.)

Late Forties: I sold more short stories! Sometimes even for good pay. Sometimes not. I began going to genre conventions, meeting more and more writers, learning more and more about How It All Works. I discovered collaborative writing, and sold a number of jointly drafted short stories. Was I published yet?

Now: *Eel River* went through both critique groups, got reworked a few times, and eventually sold to a small press, which put out an ebook edition for Kindle only. When the small press did not produce royalty statements, a print edition, or any money, I took the rights back, re-edited it AGAIN, and published it through Book View Café, in both ebook and print. It has sold upwards of several dozen copies, and received some nice reviews on Amazon. Am I published yet?

I collected my favorites of those published short stories and put out *Eastlick and Other Stories* through Book View Café. It also sold a few dozen copies. So am I published yet?

Meanwhile, I wrote a collaborative novel, *Our Lady of the Islands*, with Jay Lake. It languished in editorial revisions for a few years, and was eventually abandoned, until the book finally sold to a boutique publisher. In the interim, Jay's cancer had returned, and he was unable to work on further revisions. The boutique publisher put out a gorgeous edition; sadly, Jay died before he could see it. *Publishers Weekly* named it one of the Best Books of 2014, and gave it a starred review, as did *Library Journal*; it was a finalist for an Endeavour Award. In its first year of publication, *Our Lady* sold a total of 814 copies across ebook, hardcover, and paperback. The boutique publisher has now gone out of business, orphaning the book and its (partially written) sequel. Surely I'm published now, even if you can't buy the book...

As for the future? I had also signed a four-book deal with that same boutique publisher for the *Nightcraft* series, but, as they are gone, I am now free to make other arrangements for the entire series (which may or may not turn out to be four books). I was close to having a draft of the first book that would not too badly embarrass me, until I realized that this book was actually two books...and so the rewriting continues.

At time of press, I'm also working with a new collaborator on a new series. This one, *this one*, oh let me tell you. *This* is going to be the one that breaks in, *for real...*

Persistence, I tell you. Persistence.

Shannon Page
April, 2016
Portland, Oregon

Extended Copyright Page

SHANNON PAGE was born on Halloween night and spent her early years on a back-to-the-land commune in northern California. A childhood without television gave her a great love of the written word. At seven, she wrote her first book, an illustrated adventure starring her cat Cleo. Sadly, that story is out of print, but her work has appeared in *Clarkesworld, Interzone, Fantasy, Black Static*, Tor.com, the Proceedings of the 2002 International Oral History Association Congress, and many anthologies, including the Australian Shadows Award-winning *Grants Pass,* and *The Mammoth Book of Dieselpunk.*

Books include *Eel River;* the collection *Eastlick and Other Stories;* and *Our Lady of the Islands*, co-written with the late Jay Lake. *Our Lady* received starred reviews from *Publishers Weekly* and *Library Journal*, was named one of *Publishers Weekly*'s Best Books of 2014, and was a finalist for the Endeavour Award. Forthcoming books include *The Queen and The Tower*, first book in The Nightcraft Series; a sequel to *Our Lady;* and, writing with Karen G. Berry as Laura Gayle, *Orcas Intrigue,* the first book in the Chameleon Chronicles. Edited books include the anthology *Witches, Stitches & Bitches*, from Evil Girlfriend Media; several well-received novels from Per Aspera Press; and the essay collection *The Usual Path to Publication.*

Shannon is a longtime yoga practitioner, has no tattoos, and is an avid gardener at home with her husband, Mark Ferrari, in Portland, Oregon. She has a tiny office made from a toolshed in the backyard, where all the magic happens. Visit her at www.shannonpage.net.